"To study with Dr. Kelly Kapic is to discover how his delight in teaching theology is infectious; at the same time he is in blood earnest in believing how essential good theology is to shape minds and transform lives for the glory of God. With delightful signposts from the great theologians of the past, *A Little Book for New Theologians* guides us to a mountain of unending discovery. Here is an ideal starter kit for the beginning theology student and an affection-refresher for those who have been longer on the way."

Sinclair B. Ferguson, professor of systematic theology, Westminster Seminary, Dallas

"For many Christians the word *theology* is synonymous with *abstruse, irrelevant* and *boring*. In this jewel of a book, Kelly Kapic shows that theology is really, as the Puritan William Ames said, 'the science of living in the presence of God.' This is a great primer both for new students of theology and for those well practiced in the discipline."

Timothy George, Beeson Divinity School of Samford University

"This 'little book' is about a topic that is bigger than life, namely how to begin to think after God. Indeed, this useful manual is based on the conviction that all Christians are already engaged in a theological task as they continue wrestling with the questions of faith. Deceitfully easy and highly accessible, this guide is based on the best of theological wisdom and tested classroom experience. Highly recommended."

Veli-Matti Kärkkäinen, Fuller Theological Seminary and University of Helsinki, Finland

"Kelly Kapic concisely states major characteristics of faithful theologians in this little book. For readers who wish a brief explanation of how theology functions with reason, prayer, study, humility and repentance, this is a very good beginning. Utilizing salient insights from Augustine, Calvin, Kierkegaard and major reform theologians, he maps out the territory for thinking theologically."

Thomas C. Oden, Emeritus Henry Anson Buttz Professor of Theology, Drew University

A LITTLE BOOK FOR
NEW THEOLOGIANS

WHY AND HOW TO STUDY THEOLOGY

KELLY M. KAPIC

An imprint of InterVarsity Press
Downers Grove, Illinois

InterVarsity Press
P.O. Box 1400, Downers Grove, IL 60515-1426
World Wide Web: www.ivpress.com
E-mail: email@ivpress.com

©2012 by Kelly M. Kapic

All rights reserved. No part of this book may be reproduced in any form without written permission from InterVarsity Press.

InterVarsity Press® is the book-publishing division of InterVarsity Christian Fellowship/ USA®, a movement of students and faculty active on campus at hundreds of universities, colleges and schools of nursing in the United States of America, and a member movement of the International Fellowship of Evangelical Students. For information about local and regional activities, write Public Relations Dept., InterVarsity Christian Fellowship/USA, 6400 Schroeder Rd., P.O. Box 7895, Madison, WI 53707-7895, or visit the IVCF website at <www.intervarsity.org>.

Scripture quotations, unless otherwise noted, are from the Holy Bible, English Standard Version, copyright © 2001 by Crossway Bibles, a division of Good News Publishers. Used by permission. All rights reserved.

While all stories in this book are true, some names and identifying information in this book have been changed to protect the privacy of the individuals involved.

Interior design: Beth Hagenberg
Cover design: Cindy Kiple

ISBN 978-0-8308-3975-9

Printed in the United States of America

InterVarsity Press is committed to protecting the environment and to the responsible use of natural resources. As a member of Green Press Initiative we use recycled paper whenever possible. To learn more about the Green Press Initiative, visit <www.greenpressinitiative.org>.

Library of Congress Cataloging-in-Publication Data

Kapic, Kelly M., 1972-
  A little book for new theologians: why and how to study theology /
Kelly M. Kapic.
    p. cm.
  Includes bibliographical references and index.
  ISBN 978-0-8308-3975-9 (pbk.: alk. paper)
  1. Theology—Study and teaching.   I. Title.
BV4020.K37 2012
230.071—dc23

2012018673

P	20	19	18	17	16	15	14	13	12	11	10		
Y	28	27	26	25	24	23	22	21	20	19	18	17	16

TO DANNY KAPIC
MORE THAN A BROTHER . . .

■ ■ ■

CONTENTS

Acknowledgments 9

PART ONE
Why Study Theology?

    1. Entering the Conversation 15

    2. To Know and Enjoy God 21
       Becoming Wise

    3. Theology as Pilgrimage. 30

PART TWO
Characteristics of Faithful Theology and Theologians

    4. The Inseparability of Life and Theology 41

    5. Faithful Reason. 49

    6. Prayer and Study 64

    7. Humility and Repentance. 71

    8. Suffering, Justice and Knowing God 80

    9. Tradition and Community 93

    10. Love of Scripture 106

Name and Subject Index 122

Scripture Index 124

ACKNOWLEDGMENTS

I HAVE SEEN GOD USE good theology to liberate lives. But I have also seen people misuse theology, resulting in abuse, hard hearts and pain. One thing that I have become concerned about in theological studies is the temptation to make overly strong divisions: between academics and the church, between theology and life, between truth and love. In the past the task of theological reflection was often intertwined with the experience and character of the theologian, so that the result was an organic connection between themes like prayer, humility, suffering and community and the act of "doing" theology. My worry is that in our day, for many of us, we have unintentionally cultivated what might be called theological detachment: such a view produces a divide between spirituality and theology, between life and thought, between faith and agency. Theological detachment creates a deep misunderstanding that negatively affects not only our lives but also our theology, our churches and even the world in which we witness and serve. So here is my small offering; I hope students might read this book near the beginning of their theological studies, whether such education takes place formally within a classroom or informally as one sits reading and reflecting. My prayer is that this book might, in some small way, help new theologians avoid the strong dichotomies of theological detachment.

The heart of this little book was first written seven or so years ago, although it has undergone various revisions since its inception. My great hope and prayer is that it might serve as a kind of updated attempt at what Helmut Thielicke brilliantly accomplished in his classic, *A Little Exercise for Young Theologians*, written in 1959 and translated into English in 1962.

As I mentioned, the book in your hands has gone through many revisions, mostly because I have been using versions of it in my Doctrine 1 course at Covenant College. Countless students have given feedback and inspiration through the years, and I am sure the final version is much stronger as a result of their assistance. There are some folks in particular who read various versions of this and offered noteworthy help, feedback and encouragement: Sinclair Ferguson, Wesley Vander Lugt, Justin Borger, Brian Hecker, John Holberg, Cameron Moran, John Yates, Bill Davis, John Wingard, Jay Green, Jeff Morton, Paul Morton and Gary Deddo. Members of my department (Scott, Jeff, Dan, Herb, Ray and Ken) all provided various sorts of assistance along the way, for which I am deeply thankful.

Tabitha, my wife, remains the best theologian I know. I can't thank you enough for your faith, hope and love:

this is the soil out of which Jonathan, Margot and I grow and live. Thank you for bearing witness to God's glory in weakness, for your wisdom in times of uncertainty and for your courage amid the chaos.

Finally, I dedicate this book to Danny Kapic, my brother in flesh and in spirit. I cannot thank God enough for you. You have become a rock for me, quick to offer a listening ear, words of grace, prayers of mercy and innumerable forms of love. From our days of unbelief to the wonder of God's mercy to our families, I stand amazed at how Christ has worked. Thank you for becoming a great model to me of integrity, faith, sacrifice and promise. And thanks for always helping me to laugh—that is a wonderful gift.

PART ONE

WHY STUDY THEOLOGY?

1

ENTERING THE CONVERSATION

*We are all called theologians,
just as [we are] all [called] Christians.*
MARTIN LUTHER, "SERMON ON PSALM 5"

■ ■ ■

TELL ME ABOUT GOD.

For some people the question of whether or not God exists is a painful and haunting uncertainty not easily dismissed. But for most people the question is not whether God exists, but what is God like. Not whether there is a deity, but how many, and which one(s). How do we know God? Can God be trusted? Does God care? And is God good?

Whenever we speak about God we are engaged in theology. The term "theology" means a word (*logos*) about God (*theos*), so when anyone speaks about God, whether that person dropped out of high school or completed a PhD in philosophy, he or she is engaged in theology. Theology is not reserved for those in the academy; it is an

(divine status, quality or nature)

aspect of thought and conversation for all who live and breathe, who wrestle and fear, who hope and pray.

Theological questions surround our lives, whether we know it or not. A wife and husband facing infertility inevitably struggle through deep theological questions, whether or not they want to voice them. College students working through issues of identity, culture, politics and ethics struggle—in one way or another—with theological convictions and how to live them. Our concepts about the divine inform our lives more deeply than most people

> If I speak truth here, it is not so much knowledge that lifts me up, but rather the ardor of a burning soul that urges me to try this.
>
> Richard of St. Victor (d. 1173), "Book Three of the Trinity"

can trace. Whether we view God as distant or near, as gracious or capricious, as concerned or apathetic, the conclusions we reach—whether the result of careful reflection or negligent assumptions—guide our lives.

Christians must care deeply about theology. If the true God is renewing our lives and calling us to worship him "in spirit and truth" (Jn 4:23), then such worship includes our thoughts, words, affections and actions. Do we want to worship Yahweh or waste time and effort on a deity we have constructed in our own image? Ludwig Feuerbach (1804-1872), a nineteenth-century atheist philosopher, argued that talk about God is no more than amplified talk about ourselves: "God" is merely the projection of human thoughts and desires.[1] Surprising as it may seem, Christians share a fundamental concern with Feuerbach, for

> Whether our theology is good or flawed, those we love most will be first to feel the effects.
>
> Carolyn Custis James,
> *When Life and Beliefs Collide*

we recognize the temptation to create our own gods—gods that belong to us—rather than to respond faithfully to the One who is.

The Scriptures testify to the God who made the heavens and the earth, who created men and women to enjoy his creation and their communion with him. But sin has entered the world, creating chaos instead of order, death instead of life, and substituting idolatry for the worship of the true God. The Bible often describes our temptation to create and follow false gods. For example, after delivering Israel from Egypt, God warns them against forgetting their Redeemer and turning to false gods: "Take care lest your heart be deceived, and you turn aside and serve other gods and worship them" (Deut 11:16). The Song of Moses warns that, despite this display of God's

---

[1] Ludwig Feuerbach, *The Essence of Christianity* (1841; reprint, New York: Barnes & Noble, 2004). This line of thinking was also picked up and popularized, for example, by Sigmund Freud.

favor and power, the Israelites would eventually look to "strange gods . . . to gods they had never known, to new gods that had come recently, whom your fathers had never dreaded. You were unmindful of the Rock that bore you, and you forgot the God who gave you birth" (Deut 32:16-18). The Song warns coming generations against provoking God with their idols—with "what is no god" (Deut 32:21).

Theological reflection is a way of examining our praise, prayers, words and worship with the goal of making sure they conform to God alone. Every age has

> Praise is, among other things, a form of thinking, and aims to "think God" as adequately as possible.
>
> David Ford and Daniel W. Hardy, *Living in Praise*

its own idols, its own distortions that twist and pervert how we view God, ourselves and the world. Whether it is the distant and uninterested deity of modernity or the fragmented and territorial gods of postmodernity, all times and cultures carry the danger of warping our worship. We aim not to escape our cultures, however, but to recognize that God calls us to respond faithfully to him in our place and time, whatever our particular social and philosophical climate. We, not just our ancestors, are invited to know and love God—and thus to worship him.

While most of us are no longer drawn to the Baals and Ashtaroths of the past, we still look to idols—that which is not God—for our security, happiness and comfort. Is it not true that when many of us feel anxious or depressed, we seek relief by purchasing things: we head to the contemporary temples of self-indulgence in the malls across the country or on the Internet, where the shopping experience is meant to calm our souls? Similarly, the emphasis in American culture on comfort, which exalts the consumer over the community, skews how we view ourselves, others and creation. We lose sight of our relational nature, embracing instead the myth of individuality and autonomy. One of the greatest theological challenges of our time is to move our worship beyond self-absorption. This takes us back to Feuerbach's critique of religion: that

> Let me seek you in longing,
> and long for you in seeking.
> Let me find you in love,
> and love you in finding.
>
> Anselm (c. 1033-1109),
> *Proslogion*

we religious folks are, in the end and at the start, concerned only with ourselves. Sociologist Alan Wolfe has criticized contemporary evangelical churches for mirroring the self-centered aspects of American culture. "Television, publishing, political campaigning, education, self-help advice—all increasingly tell Americans what they already want to hear. Religion, it would seem, should now be added to that list."[2] One great danger of idols is that we try to fill our souls with what cannot satisfy, and then in our loneliness, questions and despair we wonder where God is. We were created for fellowship with God, and apart from that communion we are lost. Theology is about life, and it is not a conversation our souls can afford to avoid.

---

[2]Alan Wolfe, *The Transformation of American Religion: How We Actually Live Our Faith* (New York: Free Press, 2003), p. 36.

2

TO KNOW AND ENJOY GOD

BECOMING WISE

> *Theology is more of a virtue than an art,*
> *more wisdom than factual knowledge.*
> *It consists more in virtue and efficacy than*
> *in contemplation and knowledge.*
>
> ALEXANDER OF HALLES,
> QUOTED IN *THEOLOGICAL COMMONPLACES*

■ ■ ■

WE ENJOY GOD to the degree that we worship him faithfully. Faithful worship—including praise, prayer, obedience and faith—matters because idolatry, in whatever form, satisfies neither God nor us. Worship does not require that we perfectly understand everything about God but that we respond genuinely to the true God who makes himself known to us. The words of Saint Augustine (354-430) are as true now as they were in the fourth century when he first prayed them:

> You arouse us so that praising you may bring
> us joy,
> because you have made us and drawn us
> to yourself,
> and our heart is [restless] until it rests in you.[1]

God freely created that which was not God, and among his reasons for creating was a desire to see his creation freely reflect his glory and bask in his love. Under the warmth of his creative work and care, humanity was invited to walk with God, to know him and to love him. This is worship. But from early on there has been a power that seeks to distort our view of God, to call his provision and kindness into question. With human sin we come face to face with the realities of evil, suffering and death: this is the broader context of our brokenness. Sin creates a rupture in relationships between God and humanity, between people, between humanity and creation. Sin has clouded our view of and interaction with God, ourselves and the world. In this situation worship is impaired, confused and often lost. The gospel proclaims reconciliation in these relationships—first to God and then to his creation. Christians are called to enter into the chorus of praise that is true worship, responding in the Spirit to the revelation of the saving God in Jesus Christ. Theology is

---

[1] Augustine, *The Confessions* 1.1, trans. Maria Boulding, *The Works of Saint Augustine: A Translation for the Twenty-First Century*, ed. John E. Rotelle (Brooklyn, N.Y.: New City Press, 1997), I/1:39. I have here replaced her translation of "unquiet" with the more classic rendering, "restless."

all about knowing how to sing the song of redemption: to know when to shout, when to mourn, when to be silent and when to hope. But in order to enjoy the song and sing it well, we must learn the words and the music.

Ignatius of Antioch (d. 117), who died by the mauling of beasts in a Roman arena not many years after the death

> Theologies that cannot be sung (or prayed for that matter) are certainly wrong at a deep level, and such theologies leave me, in both senses, cold: cold-hearted and uninterested.
>
> J. I. Packer, *God Has Spoken*

of the apostles, wrote seven challenging letters to churches being pressed to alter or abandon their worship of Jesus Christ. He said, "Study, therefore, to be established in the doctrines of the Lord and the apostles, that so all things, whatsoever you do, may prosper both in the flesh and spirit; in faith and love; in the Son, and in the Father, and in the Spirit."[2] Rather than compromise his worship of God, Ignatius was willing to face death—and his knowledge of God sustained him. Writing more than a century later, Lactantius (250-324) similarly concluded that "the knowledge of God comes first, His worship is the result of

---

[2]Ignatius, "Epistle of Ignatius to Magnesians," in *Ante-Nicene Fathers*, ed. A. Roberts and J. Donaldson (Peabody, Mass.: Hendrickson, 1994), 1:64. "Ye" is changed to "you" here for contemporary readers.

knowledge."[3] When one begins to know God in his beauty and truth, worship springs into being. Having said that, even as we worship, our knowledge not only grows but also is often revised and reshaped. Worship and knowledge are interrelated. There is reciprocity between the two; they are not simply one-way streets. But how do we understand what or whom we are worshiping?

"Knowledge" in theology is not merely cognitive but also personal with elements of connection and commitment. It would be a dangerous misunderstanding to as-

> He who understands Him best loves and praises him best.
>
> Teresa of Ávila (1515-1582),
> *The Life of Teresa of Jesus*

sert that we can only worship God once we have understood all the important doctrines. The relationship between worship and knowing is not that one-dimensional. Augustine of Hippo, already mentioned, argued that rationality might be considered glorious, but there was something greater than reason: he called this "the truth" (i.e., Christ himself). Only in relation to this truth can we experience real enjoyment (see Jn 14:7; 17:3; 20:31; Mt 11:27; 1 Jn 5:20). "Our freedom is found in submission to this truth. And it is our God Himself who frees us

---

[3]Lactantius, *The Divine Institutes* 4.4, in *Ante-Nicene Fathers*, ed. A. Roberts and J. Donaldson (Peabody, Mass.: Hendrickson, 1994), 7:104.

from death, namely, our sinful condition. . . . *But the soul is not free in the enjoyment of anything unless it is secure in that enjoyment."*[4] Knowledge and enjoyment of God are inseparable.

The sixteenth-century reformer John Calvin (1509-1564) similarly connected knowledge to worship. He argues for a strong relationship between our knowledge of God and our knowledge of ourselves, both of which are vital for faithful worship. Calvin begins his *Institutes of the Christian Religion* with these words: "Nearly all the wisdom we possess, that is to say, true and sound wisdom, consists of two parts: the knowledge of God and of ourselves. But, while joined by many bonds, which one precedes and brings forth the other is not easy to discern."[5]

In other words, there is a strong relationship between knowing God and knowing ourselves: while Calvin will argue we should start with the former (knowing God), he does not think the task is complete without moving to the latter (knowing ourselves).[6] We can never rightly understand ourselves, our meaning or true human satisfaction

---

[4]Augustine, *The Free Choice of the Will* 2.6.11-12, reproduced in Paul Helm, *Faith and Reason*, Oxford Readers (Oxford: Oxford University Press, 1999), pp. 65-69, emphasis added.

[5]John Calvin, *Institutes of the Christian Religion*, ed. John T. McNeill, trans. Ford Lewis Battles, 2 vols., Library of Christian Classics (Philadelphia: Westminster Press, 1960), 1.1.1-2.

[6]He writes, "Yet, however the knowledge of God and of ourselves may be mutually connected, the order of right teaching requires that we discuss the former first, then proceed afterward to treat the latter." Calvin, *Institutes* 1.1.1.

apart from knowing God. True worship—and true wisdom—comes not through an exercise in autonomous introspection but by presenting ourselves humbly to the living God. The knowledge of God and knowledge of self grow within this fellowship: we can never properly understand ourselves if we attempt to do this apart from knowing God.

Growing in our knowledge of God changes our view of everything else. It is not that we lose sight of all except God, but rather that we view everything in light of God and through the story of his creation and redemption.[7] True worship of God frees and enables us to love his creation rightly and to grieve when we see it abused. Further, our worship has its impulse from a future hope as

> The fear of the LORD is the beginning of wisdom;
> all those who practice it have a good understanding.
>
> Psalm 111:10

well as the records of God's past actions: the risen Christ will return, bringing the fullness of his kingdom and eternal, unhindered communion with God.

This knowledge is all-encompassing. True worship is not restricted to congregational gatherings, but it inhabits the whole of our existence. This is partly why worship is

---

[7]Helmut Thielicke, *I Believe: The Christian's Creed* (Philadelphia: Fortress, 1968), p. 7.

To Know and Enjoy God 27

tied to wisdom. The "fear of the Lord," spoken of throughout Scripture, is not normally meant to convey the idea of being frightened. Rather, it carries the idea of awe and wonder, of joy and hope. The fear of the Lord is "the beginning of wisdom," not because a person immediately understands archaic Latin phrases and complex mathematics, but because the worshiper no longer sees only a fragmented world, but stands before the One who holds all things together (see Prov 1:7; 2:1-6; 9:10; Ps 19:9; 111:10). Fearing the Lord means that we are not left to our own resources to control and survive the elements of creation, but that we can trust the Creator who sustains that creation, controls the future and has our best interests at heart (e.g., Prov 23:17-18). This wisdom allows believers to sing the full song of redemption rather than merely disconnected stanzas.

What distinguishes the wise from the foolish in Scripture is how they respond to God's Word and work. Where foolish persons demand that God must work within the parameters of their limited understanding, wise persons expand and readjust their views to fit God's words, work and creation. The foolish person lives as though individuals can decide whether or not God exists, and if he does exist, what God's activities can be like (Ps 14:1-7; 92:5-6; 53:1; cf. 1 Cor 1:18-31). The wise person recognizes the limits of human reason and perception and therefore delights in the fact that the eternal One has unveiled himself and has invited us to know and abide with him.

> How precious to me are your thoughts, O God!
> How vast is the sum of them!
> If I would count them, they are more than
>   the sand.
> I awake, and I am still with you. (Ps 139:17-18)

The songs of the psalmists capture in poetic form the connection between fearing and delighting in God. What an overwhelming thought to recognize that the eternal God who created all things is the same God who "takes pleasure in his people" (Ps 149:4). God "takes pleasure in those who fear him, in those who hope in his steadfast love" (Ps 147:11). Our "heart is glad in him" who is our help and shield, for not only is Yahweh holy and powerful, but also his love rests upon his people (Ps 33:20-22). Since God delights in his people and has the power to protect them, it should be no surprise that the Scriptures call us to delight in God and promise that we can rest in God as our sanctuary.

> God is our refuge and strength,
> a very present help in trouble.
> Therefore we will not fear though the earth
>   gives way,
> though the mountains be moved into the heart
>   of the sea,
> though its waters roar and foam,
> though the mountains tremble at its swelling. . . .
> "Be still, and know that I am God.
> I will be exalted among the nations,

I will be exalted in the earth!"
The LORD of hosts is with us;
the God of Jacob is our fortress. (Ps 46:1-3, 10-11)

By coming to the living God with our life, questions, fears and hopes, we grow in our knowledge of God. This

> The proper end of the drama of doctrine is wisdom: lived knowledge, a performance of the truth.
>
> Kevin J. Vanhoozer,
> *The Drama of Doctrine*

knowledge is not merely intellectual; it is also passionate, touching both our understanding and affections.

Our approach to God challenges us to "think God's thoughts after him." Although our understanding is never final, and although we can expect that we will misunderstand or misapply aspects of what we learn, he still invites us to begin.[8] And thus, with eyes lifted toward him we live, speak and praise. This is the beginning of the fear of the Lord; this is the beginning of wisdom; this is the beginning of worship.

---

[8]Herman Bavinck, *Reformed Dogmatics: Prolegomena*, ed. John Bolt, trans. John Vriend (Grand Rapids: Baker Academic, 2003), p. 44.

3

THEOLOGY AS PILGRIMAGE

*People have fallen into a foolish habit of speaking
of orthodoxy as something heavy, humdrum, and safe.
There never was anything so perilous or
so exciting as orthodoxy.*

G. K. CHESTERTON, *ORTHODOXY*

■ ■ ■

WE ARE NOT GOD. This may seem ridiculously obvious, but much of our practice ignores this simple truth. Not only can we not control the events around us, but our understanding is inescapably incomplete. Human reflections about God are always limited by at least two key realities: our finitude and our sin. Although few Christians explicitly deny these realities, sometimes we act as though our theological reflections are free from these factors.

While medieval and early Protestant theologians often wrote in technical ways that sound foreign or esoteric to contemporary Christians, these theologians make dis-

Theology as Pilgrimage 31

tinctions that remain helpful. One such distinction is between *archetypal* and *ectypal* knowledge of God.[1]

Archetypal knowledge of God is that knowledge by which God perfectly knows himself. Neither finitude nor sin limits him. He knows all things. Most centrally, God fully knows himself.

> The truth is not in the middle, and not in one extreme, but in both extremes.
>
> Charles Simeon, quoted in John Stott, *Christ the Controversialist*

Ectypal knowledge is that understanding we have of God by means of his self-revelation, which is most clearly stated in Scripture and has its high point in the incarnation of the Word.

Thus we can have true knowledge of God, although it is incomplete knowledge. Even with divinely given Scripture, finite and sinful humanity needs the illumination of the Holy Spirit to understand it rightly and accept its message. Ectypal knowledge depends on the work of the Holy Spirit to reveal the Word to our minds and to seal the Word to our hearts.[2] It is important to recognize the trini-

---

[1] For background, see Richard A. Muller, *Post-Reformation Reformed Dogmatics*, vol. 1, *Prolegomena to Theology* (Grand Rapids: Baker, 1993), pp. 225-38.

[2] John Calvin, *Institutes of the Christian Religion*, ed. John T. McNeill, trans. Ford Lewis Battles, 2 vols., Library of Christian Classics (Philadelphia: Westminster Press, 1960), 3.2.7; Alvin Plantinga, *Warranted Christian Belief* (New York: Oxford University Press, 2000), pp. 251-52.

tarian pattern here: the Father reveals himself through his Word as he comes to us by his Spirit (Jn 3:34-35; Rom 8:11; Phil 3:3).[3] God reveals himself through himself.[4] To know God is to know the One who comes in Word and Spirit. Yet a distinction between God and us remains: God's knowledge of himself is pure and full, while our knowledge of him is derivative and incomplete.

Because our knowledge of God must grow over time as we walk with him, it should not be surprising that some of the best imagery used to depict the theological

> All men and women exist in a state of epistemological pilgrimage.
>
> Paul Helm,
> *Faith and Understanding*

enterprise is that of pilgrimage. Biblically we read of Christians described as those who belong to "the Way" (e.g., Acts 9:2; 19:19, 23; 24:14, 22), for they are "sojourners" (1 Pet 2:11) called to "walk" by the Spirit who brings light even amid the presence of darkness (e.g., 2 Cor 5:7; Gal 5:16, 25; Eph 5:8, 15; Col 2:6; 1 Jn 1:6-7; 2 Jn 6). Drawing on such images, another classic distinction may prove useful. On the one hand, there is the imperfect theology of

---

[3] Cf. Herman Bavinck, *Reformed Dogmatics: Prolegomena*, ed. John Bolt, trans. John Vriend (Grand Rapids: Baker Academic, 2003), pp. 213-14; cf. p. 233.

[4] Cf. Karl Barth, *Church Dogmatics 1:1*, ed. G. W. Bromiley and T. F. Torrance, trans. G. W. Bromiley, 4 vols. (Edinburgh: T & T Clark, 1957-1969), p. 296.

pilgrims (*theologia viatorum*) who walk the path of faith and hope; on the other hand, there is the unblemished theology of the blessed (*theologia beatorum*) who are now with God in glory. We have knowledge now, but it is not what it will one day be. Gregory of Nazianzus (330-390) commented on the progress of the Christian's knowledge: "Of God himself the knowledge we shall have in this life will be little, though soon after it will perhaps be more perfect."[5] Saint Augustine also argued that we offer praise to God both in our present broken world and in our future paradise when sin will no longer cloud our vision. The praise offered now comes from those laden with anxiety, while in heaven all are free from concern; here there is hope, in glory "hope is realized." Augustine calls us to sing as we make our journey of faith: sing "not for pleasure as we rest, but to cheer us in our labor. As pilgrims are wont to sing, sing, and travel on. . . . If you are making progress you are marching on; but progress in good, progress in the true faith, progress in right living—sing, and travel on!"[6]

Sometimes as theologians we find ourselves climbing sun-drenched mountains or descending into dark valleys; occasionally we are rewarded with an endless vista,

---

[5] Gregory of Nazianzus, Oration 27.10, in *On God and Christ: The Five Theological Orations and Two Letters to Cledonius*, trans. Frederick Williams and Lionel R. Wickham (Crestwood, N.Y.: St. Vladimir's Seminary Press, 2002), p. 34.

[6] Augustine, Sermon 256.3, cited in Thomas A. Hand, *Augustine on Prayer*, new ed. (New York: Catholic Book Publishing, 1986), pp. 55-56.

while at other moments fog surrounds us and obscures our path. As with most long journeys, there will be times when we must stop to catch our breath, times when we may get lost and when we will do well to ask others for

> By knowing God we come to love him, and by loving him we come to know him.
>
> Ellen T. Charry,
> *By the Renewing of Your Minds*

directions. Sometimes we take paths which do not take us where we expected, while at other times we turn a corner only to discover a wonderful view that we have been longing and struggling to reach.

Pilgrimage imagery, as noted above, is used in Scripture to describe those who approach their God and gain strength from knowing his presence (e.g., Ps. 84:5-7). It is noteworthy that believers follow him who is described as "the Way"—the one who can alone lead us to the Father (Jn 14:6). Johannes Cocceius (1603-1669), a creative biblical theologian of the seventeenth century, spoke of our endeavors as "the theology of the way," and his contemporary Johannes Wollebius (1586-1629) spoke of our theological reflections as those "of the wayfarers" or pilgrims.[7] We are on an adventure; we are going some-

---

[7]Johannes Wollebius, "Compendium Theologiae Christianae," in *Reformed Dogmatics: Seventeenth-Century Reformed Theology Through the Writings of Wollebius, Voetius and Turretin*, ed. John W. Beardslee

where, so to speak, as we more faithfully witness and are conformed to God and his glory. "Now I know in part; then I shall know fully, even as I have been fully known" (1 Cor 13:12).

Our knowledge of God and our theological reflections are unavoidably finite, derivative and under development. Much of the historical commentary on cognitive limits in theology has been guided by reflections on Exodus 33:17-23. In this passage, Moses asks to see God's glory, which God allows by showing the leader of Israel his back. Since Moses could not see God's pure majesty and live, he protects Moses from the unmediated glory of his face. John Owen (1616-1683), one of the finest theologians England ever produced, found this passage helpful in framing the theological endeavor. Although Owen believed that his life was well spent by devoting his energy to proclaiming the truths of God, he was also quick to acknowledge the infinite gap between his understanding and God's reality. Drawing from Exodus 33–34, Owen concludes: "We speak much of God . . . the truth is, we know very little of him." He later adds, "We may love, honour, believe, and obey our Father; and therewith he accepts our childish thoughts, for they are but childish. We see but his back parts."[8] There will

---

III (New York: Oxford University Press, 1965), p. 29; Johannes Cocceius, "De Theologia, Ejus Tradendae Methodo [Biblical Method of Covenant Theology]," in *Reformed Reader: A Sourcebook in Christian Theology*, ed. William Stacy Johnson and John H. Leith (Louisville: Westminster/John Knox, 1993), p. 12.

[8]John Owen, *The Works of John Owen*, ed. William H. Goold, 24 vols.

come a time when we see God "as he is," but that time is yet to come (1 Jn 3:2).

It is vital to recognize that one should not give up on theology because of our limitations, for our confidence

> We know so little of God, because it is God who is thus to be known.
>
> John Owen, *Mortification of Sin*

ultimately rests on God, not on ourselves. In this sense we recognize and delight in the axiom drawn from the brilliant medieval theologian Thomas Aquinas: "Theology is taught by God, teaches of God and leads to God" (*Theologia a Deo docetur, Deum docet, et ad Deum ducit*).[9] All good and faithful theology comes from God, who is the ultimate theologian—the only one who can, without weakness or misunderstanding, speak of himself.

Jesus Christ, God with us, makes it clear that he does not simply know the truth, but rather *he* is the truth, the way and the life. Jesus, the Son of God, is really and actually God with us. He is God's great self-revelation. None can come to or know the Father but through the revelation of the Son (Jn 14:6-7). We recognize that there is an intimate knowledge shared between the Father and the Son that comes to us only by means of divine self-disclo-

---

(Edinburgh and London: Johnstone & Hunter, 1850-1855), 6:64, 65.
[9]Though often quoted, in truth these commonly repeated phrases seem to be a gathered summary of what Thomas says in *Summa Theologica* 1.1.7, where he discusses if God is the object of theology.

Theology as Pilgrimage

sure. As Jesus declares, "No one knows the Son except the Father, and no one knows the Father except the Son and *anyone to whom the Son chooses to reveal him*" (Mt 11:27,

> We cannot "know" God in a way that explains everything about him. The only way that we can approach God is through worship: holy, holy, holy.
>
> Eugene H. Peterson, *Christ Plays in Ten Thousand Places*

emphasis added). Clearly, "knowing" in this context is not merely referring to cognitive assent. *Our call is to come, to gaze at Christ, to hear his word and to respond in faith and love*. Here theology and worship come together: we are answering the call of our heavenly Father to speak words from the basis of an intimate knowledge of the Word, which is possible only by the gift of the Spirit. Theology is wrapped up in this response to God's call. Hence, it is to be faith-full: faith is always required for genuine theology. We rightly respond to God's revelation when our words about God, whether many or few, are placed into the matrix of worship. When we see the relationship between theology and worship we are moved beyond intellectual curiosity to an engaged encounter with the living God.

PART TWO

CHARACTERISTICS OF FAITHFUL THEOLOGY AND THEOLOGIANS

4

THE INSEPARABILITY OF LIFE AND THEOLOGY

*It is through living, indeed through dying
and being damned that one becomes a theologian,
not through understanding, reading, or speculation.*

MARTIN LUTHER, *OPERATIONES IN PSALMOS*

■ ■ ■

THEOLOGICAL REFLECTION is a deeply personal venture; it does not leave room for cool scientific detachment.[1] At its best theology may be considered both an art and a science. Here we encounter the beauty and holiness of God, and such an encounter is always emotive, whether we realize it or not, whether we want it to be or not. We do not stand off in the distance as neutral observers, but rather we are engaged as those who wrestle with and rest in the God who has made himself known. The Reformers

---

[1] Cf. Michael Polanyi, *Personal Knowledge: Towards a Post-Critical Philosophy* (Chicago: University of Chicago Press, 1962). All affirmations have an unavoidably personal reality to them. The Enlightenment goal of impersonal, objective knowledge was a mirage, and an undesirable one at that.

were willing to call theology a science, as long as it was understood as a practical science (*scientia practica*) rather than a speculative one (*scientia speculativa*). William Ames (1576-1633) defined theology as the "teaching [*doctrina*] of living to God."[2] He understood that true theology is inevitably *lived* theology. Given this reciprocal activity between reflection and life, I believe that there are certain elements which should accompany any good theologian and theology. Attempting to separate life and theology is to lose the beauty and truthfulness of both.

How is my life related to my theology? It is a fairly modern notion to separate theology as a science from theology as a practical reflection on life. Only in the last four hundred years have people tended to treat them as distinct disciplines rather than as interwoven activities.[3] Notice how often the structure of Pauline letters in the New Testament, for example, moves from the indicative to the imperative, from theological observations to practical application. The interplay between theological theory and Christian living is similar to the relationship between hermeneutical theory and our current prejudices and expectations. Christians can agree with the postmodern critiques claiming that it is naïve to try to separate one's

---

[2]William Ames, *The Marrow of Theology*, ed. John Dykstra Eusden (Grand Rapids: Baker Books, 1997), p. 77.

[3]David Clyde Jones, *Biblical Christian Ethics* (Grand Rapids: Baker, 1994), p. 7. See also the excellent survey by Brian Brock, "Christian Ethics," in *Mapping Modern Theology: A Thematic and Historical Introduction*, ed. Kelly M. Kapic and Bruce L. McCormack (Grand Rapids: Baker Academic, 2012), chap. 12.

The Inseparability of Life and Theology

experience from one's interpretation of the world, of oneself or even of texts. The church has always recognized elements of this claim. Scripture adopts the perspective that our sin corrupts our interpretations of reality. It also confesses—in contrast to postmodern critiques—that with the Spirit's help people can understand the truth of God. Paul puts it this way:

> But, as it is written, "What no eye has seen, nor ear heard, nor the heart of man imagined, what God has prepared for those who love him"—these things God has revealed to us through the Spirit. For the Spirit searches everything, even the depths of God. For who knows a person's thoughts except the spirit of that person, which is in him? So also no one comprehends the thoughts of God except the Spirit of God. Now we have received not the spirit of the world, but the Spirit who is from God, that we might understand the things freely given us by God. And we impart this in words not taught by human wisdom but taught by the Spirit, interpreting spiritual truths to those who are spiritual. (1 Cor 2:9-13; cf. Job 32:8-9)

Both our theological constructions and our practical convictions are subject to the superintending work of the Holy Spirit.

When Gregory of Nazianzus (330-390) found himself engaged in difficult discussions about the nature of the triune God, he unhesitatingly argued that life and theology are inseparable. Religion is trivialized, Gregory warned, when one approaches theology obsessed with "setting and solving conundrums," rather than with an attitude of worship. For Gregory, ideal theologians were those set apart not only by rigorous study but also through spiritual preparation; for "one who is not pure to lay hold of pure things is dangerous, just as it is for weak eyes to

> Christianity is dogmatical, devotional, practical all at once; it is esoteric and exoteric; it is indulgent and strict; it is light and dark; it is love, and it is fear.
>
> John Henry Newman, *An Essay on the Development of Christian Doctrine*

look at the sun's brightness."[4] Here we are reminded of Jesus' beatitude, "Blessed are the pure in heart, for they shall see God" (Mt 5:8). Here the point is not arrogant self-righteousness but humble sensitivity and response to God's presence. Gregory often pointed out that theological discussion is not the same thing as true theology, nor is a theological discussion a substitute for knowing God.

Fifteen hundred years later, Princeton theologian Charles Hodge (1797-1878) made the same connection between life and theology. Although his methodology was scientific and logical, Hodge did not divorce it from per-

---

[4]Gregory of Nazianzus, Oration 27.3, in *On God and Christ: The Five Theological Orations and Two Letters to Cledonius*, trans. Frederick Williams and Lionel R. Wickham (Crestwood, N.Y.: St. Vladimir's Seminary Press, 2002), p. 27; see pp. 25-35.

sonal attachment to God. Talking to an audience of theological students, Hodge tied piety to theology, arguing that bad theology often grows out of dying religious feelings: "if a man's religious opinions are the result and expression of his religious feelings, if *heterodoxy be the consequence rather than the cause of the loss of piety*, then 'keep your hearts with all diligence, for out of them are the issues of life' (Prov. 4:23, KJV)." We often think that theology becomes defective because of faulty thinking. Not so, argues Hodge. Our theology can become corrupted because we neglect to attend to our lives, for true theology

> Christians learn doctrine in order to participate more deeply, passionately, and truthfully in the drama of redemption. Intellectual apprehension alone, without the appropriation of heart and hand, leads only to hypocrisy.
>
> Kevin J. Vanhoozer, *The Drama of Doctrine*

must always be true spirituality. He concludes, "Holiness is essential to correct knowledge of divine things, and the great security from error."[5] While Hodge, of all people, was not naïve about the intellectually demanding task of

---

[5] Charles Hodge, "Lecture to Theological Students," in *The Princeton Theology, 1812-1921: Scripture, Science and Theological Method from Archibald Alexander to Benjamin Breckinridge Warfield*, ed. Mark A. Noll (Grand Rapids: Baker Academic, 2001), p. 112.

theological exploration, he recognized that cognitive reflection always occurs within the context of experience. The goal here is not perfection or some strange attempt at spirituality defined by ever-increasing attempts of self-improvement. A pious and holy person is not one who is free from the struggle with sin but one who freely soaks in the love of the Father and the grace of the Son and

> The person who speaks [of] God and divine matters [but does so] not from love of God and for God's glory is not able to speak God truly, for he does not really know him and does not speak from God and in God.
>
> Johannes Cocceius,
> *Summa Theologiae*

finds renewal in the strong fellowship of the Spirit. Simply talking about God does not make one pious.

Given the reciprocal relationship between theology and practice, it becomes imperative that theologians, whether armchair or professional, cultivate faithfulness. J. I. Packer has warned us, "If our theology does not quicken the conscience and soften the heart, it actually hardens both; if it does not encourage the commitment of faith, it reinforces the detachment of unbelief; if it fails to promote humility, it inevitably feeds pride."[6] Pride and

---

[6]J. I. Packer, *A Quest for Godliness: The Puritan Vision of the Christian Life* (Wheaton, Ill.: Crossway, 1990), p. 15.

arrogance, which often accompany theological discussion, are not simply the temptation of the domineering pastor or condescending professor; they are a temptation for all of us. When we speak of God, a strange enticement can occur. In subtle ways we begin to confuse ourselves with God. We think our words, our understanding, our convictions perfectly reflect God's truth. In fact, we are not God, we have blind spots, we do not ever fully see how all things work together. Marks of a corrupted theology include fits of anger, jealousy, division and strife (Gal 5:19-21), where understanding has become an idol rather than an avenue to the living God. Genuine theology cultivates a spirituality of grace, humility, truth, gentleness, unity, peace, patience and love (Gal 5:22-26). To separate theology and spirituality is to misunderstand, and eventually damage, both.

What I am advocating here is what I have elsewhere called an anthroposensitive theology, by which I mean *a refusal to divorce theological considerations from practical human application, since theological reflections are always interwoven with anthropological concerns.*[7] This combination of "anthropo-" ("human"; "relating to human beings"; from Greek *anthrōpos*) and "sensitive" is an attempt to avoid an overly simplistic classification of theology as either theocentric (God-centered) or anthropocentric (human-centered).

---

[7] See Kelly M. Kapic, *Communion with God: The Divine and the Human in the Theology of John Owen* (Grand Rapids: Baker Academic, 2007). Some of the wording from this paragraph comes directly from pp. 33-34.

Clearly our theology must be God-centered, but this language can mask the reality that our theology is, at the same time, concerned with our relation to this God. While other terms such as "pastoral" or "experiential" could be used, these terms often carry either unnecessarily negative connotations or represent a notion of what is done only *after* theological reflection, as though we work to get our theology correct and then move on to practical concerns. Yet in the complex relationship between life and theology, we should admit that for good or ill our experience and practice not only grow out of our theology but also inform it. With this in mind, we turn our attention to characteristics that we must cultivate as the appropriate context for our theological activity:

- faithful reason
- prayer and study
- humility and repentance
- suffering, justice and knowing God
- tradition and community
- love of Scripture

5

FAITHFUL REASON

For if you do not come, you do not see;
if you do not see, neither do you believe;
if you do not believe, you are still standing far off.
But if you believe, you come near,
and if you believe, you see.

AUGUSTINE, "EXPOSITION OF THE PSALMS"

■ ■ ■

NATIONAL PUBLIC RADIO recently ran a series entitled "This I Believe." Once a week NPR played recordings of short essays read by a variety of people, including politicians, religious leaders, artists and teenagers. The essays explored what was central to people's lives—what gives them meaning, guides their convictions and strengthens them when times are difficult. Amid such public discourse various questions arise, such as, "What is a good foundation for your life?"

Along these lines, it is common for theological works, especially those in the tradition of the Enlightenment, to spend considerable time on the "prolegomena" to theology, in other words, on assumptions and considerations that we must examine before starting to dig into theology itself. One of these is the question of the relationship between faith and reason. Is not unbiased reason the only thing that can provide a sure foundation to build on? Some argue that a person can legitimately discuss theology only after independent "reasonable evidence" has been produced to demonstrate that there is a God and that certain things can be known about him. In other words, they claim, it is unjustifiable to speak about God until one first establishes that such speech does not violate the canons of rationality. To believe, apart from recognized evidence, offends the sensibilities of some who are trained within the assumptions of modernity. In their method, one normally moves from humanity to God, attempting to reason up a ladder to see if one can reach the heavens.

> In its own way, theology is a science, whose conclusions necessarily follow from their principles; but those principles are articles of faith, and faith itself is an assent to the word of God accepted as word of God.
>
> Etienne Gilson, *Reason and Revelation in the Middle Ages*

Behind questions about the relationship between faith and reason are concerns about authority and knowledge. How do we know what we know? What—or who—gives us the authority to say we know anything; and what is our relationship to this thing or person? Responding to such questions, it seems appropriate to highlight God's character and his revelatory action rather than to begin solely with notions about human rationality. This is not meant to disparage reason but only to put it in its proper place as one begins theological studies.

In practice, some kind of faith commitment—a trust we place in something—is essential to all thinking. We never use our powers of reasoning without first placing our trust somewhere. Whether talking about mundane matters of daily life or religious conclusions with eternal consequences, faith in something will come before our theorizing. Roy A. Clouser has convincingly argued for the pervasive and inescapable role of "religious belief" in all of our theories, even when such theories (e.g., radical materialism) seem to deny the very existence of God.[1] It is impossible to escape certain commitments which inevitably must be described as faith. But our concern here is not about the faith one has in the assumed order of the universe or about the trust a person places in his or her dog's ability to retrieve the newspaper. Rather, we are specifically concerned about rightly understanding the role of

---

[1] Roy A. Clouser, *The Myth of Religious Neutrality: An Essay on the Hidden Role of Religious Belief in Theories*, rev. ed. (Notre Dame: University of Notre Dame Press, 2005). He defines "religious belief" in the following manner: "A religious belief is any belief in something or other as divine. 'Divine' means having the status of not depending on anything else" (p. 23). He uses theories in mathematics, physics and psychology to validate his argument (see chaps. 7–9).

rational reflection and the place of faith when one speaks about the God of Abraham, Isaac, Mary and Paul.

In theology, reason rightly works in the service of faith; and because of this, faithful theology does not despise rational reflection. "There is a two-way movement in theology, faith in search of understanding (*fides quaerens intellectuam*) and understanding faith (*intellectus quaerens fidem*). *Intellectus* without *fides* leads to rationalism; *fides* without *intellectus* falls into emotionalism."[2] Because all reason requires faith, we cannot choose between them; rather, we embrace reason that is faithful to God. There is a long history of those who have followed the "faith seeking understanding" method and have developed this project in a variety of ways. What unites these efforts is a commitment to begin with divine revelation rather than

> We are speaking not of an irrational leap into the unknown, but of the responsible acceptance of a personal invitation: "Follow me."
>
> Lesslie Newbigin, *Truth and Authority in Modernity*

merely self-enlightenment. The faith to receive and submit to divine revelation is not acquired at the conclusion of a syllogistic exercise; it is a gift from God.

---

[2]Carl E. Braaten, "First Locus: Prolegomena to Christian Dogmatics," in *Christian Dogmatics*, ed. Carl E. Braaten and Robert W. Jenson (Philadelphia: Fortress, 1984), p. 18.

Augustine's model for the relationship between faith and reason is pivotal here, and a brief survey of some key statements by this early church father will demonstrate his fundamental approach. Struggling with the question of the freedom of the will and the reality of human sin, Augustine exhibits both confidence and humility: "God will help us, and make us understand what we believe. We can be sure we are treading in the path pointed out by the Prophet who says: 'Unless you believe you will not understand.'"[3] Faith is not optional for genuine understanding—it is essential and presupposed, since "our hearts need to be cleansed first by believing, that we may be able to see with them."[4] Augustine does not despise reason, claiming that it is this faculty which essentially distinguishes humanity from the animal creation. In Augustine's mind, the gift of reason is a key to understanding what it means to be made distinctly in God's image.[5] Yet the Fall has had se-

---

[3] Augustine, *The Problem of Free Choice* 1.2.4, trans. Dom Mark Pontifex (New York: Newman Press, 1955), p. 38. This quote is one of Augustine's favorites, which he roughly borrows from Isaiah 7:9, though he uses a "mistranslation" of the text, but the one available to him (see Augustine, *The Trinity* 7.12, trans. Edmund Hill, *The Works of Saint Augustine: A Translation for the Twenty-First Century*, ed. John E. Rotelle [Brooklyn, N.Y.: New City Press, 1991], I/5:232, 236 n. 50).

[4] Augustine, *Expositions of the Psalms 33–50*, trans. Maria Boulding, *The Works of St. Augustine: A Translation for the Twenty-First Century*, ed. John E. Rotelle (Brooklyn, N.Y.: New City Press, 2000), III/16:303 (Psalm 44:25).

[5] Augustine, *On Genesis: A Refutation of the Manichees* 1.28, trans. Edmund Hill, *The Works of St. Augustine: A Translation for the Twenty-First Century*, ed. John E. Rotelle (Brooklyn, N.Y.: New City Press,

vere consequences on humanity, including impairing our abilities to conceive of God rightly and respond appropriately through worship. Sin turns us in on ourselves and sadly narrows our world. Faith is necessary because, like the fear of the Lord, faith expands our horizon, whereas a rejection of faith closes down inquiry and possible knowledge. Consequently, "just because a thing is not yet clear to our understanding, we must not therefore dismiss it from the firm assent of our faith."[6] Failure to adopt a similar view would allow only those with the most impressive cognitive abilities to have access to God, and as Augustine asked with a grin, "Who knows if you are numbered among such an elite?"[7] Augustine dismisses as irrational and unsustainable any claim that belief must always begin with reason; instead, belief is a prerequisite for understanding, especially when it comes to relating to the triune God.[8] Simply put, Augustine calls us to recognize the complex relationship between our properly functioning reason and faith. There should be no denial of the objective reality and truth of God and the intelligibility of his revelation,

---

2002), I/13:57. While I think this is an overly narrow approach to understanding the "image of God," our concern here is the significance Augustine gives to human reason.

[6]Augustine, *The Trinity* 8.1, I/5:242.

[7]Augustine, *On the Profit of Believing* 24, in *A Select Library of the Nicene and Post-Nicene Fathers of the Christian Church*, ed. Philip Schaff et al. (Peabody, Mass.: Hendrickson, 1994), 1.3:358.

[8]This argument is laid out in detail by John Rist, "Faith and Reason," in *The Cambridge Companion to Augustine*, ed. Eleonore Stump and Norman Kretzmann (Cambridge: Cambridge University Press, 2001), pp. 26-39.

yet we must also take into account the web of human subjectivity, finitude and sin. We know God, but such knowledge requires faith.

I am advocating here an approach that might be called *faithful reason*. Our approach to God must acknowledge that our reason works properly only when it is full of

> The secret things belong to the LORD our God, but the things that are revealed belong to us and to our children forever.
>
> Deuteronomy 29:29

faith. Reason apart from faith is empty, just as faith apart from reason can be blind and lead toward idolatry. Faith must precede reflection for true Christian theology to occur.[9] God alone, as he has revealed himself, must be our firm foundation, and in particular, Jesus Christ, as he is made known through the apostles and prophets (1 Cor 3:10-16; Eph 2:20; cf. Lk 24:25-27). This is a foundation different from—although sometimes wrongly confused with—the recently chastened philosophical approach known as strong foundationalism.[10] The apostle Paul

---

[9]Braaten, "First Locus: Prolegomena to Christian Dogmatics," p. 17.
[10]For a critique of classical or strong foundationalism, see Nicholas Wolterstorff, "Can Belief in God Be Rational If It Has No Foundations?" in *Christian Perspectives on Religious Knowledge*, ed. C. Stephen Evans and Merold Westphal (Grand Rapids: Eerdmans, 1993); Nicholas Wolterstorff, *Reason Within the Bounds of Religion* (Grand Rapids: Eerdmans, 1976).

speaks not of independent non-reductive rational principles but rather of the trustworthy self-disclosure of God and the sinful human tendency toward suppressing God's revelation (Rom 1:18-32). Faith, by God's grace, is what allows us to see beyond ourselves to God.

Throughout the Bible faith is the response to Yahweh's revelation. The content of this faith is not merely subjective but grows out of God's revelation in word and event. God speaks and acts, and then people respond in faith. Examples abound: Abraham leaves the country of his youth to follow Yahweh's call (Gen 12:1-4), and the Syrian commander Naaman turns from his native pagan deities to the God of Israel after seeing his power and grace (2 Kings 5). God repeatedly makes himself known through word and deed to his people, and the faithful are those who respond by clinging to him and affirming his character and glory even amid difficult and painful times (Heb 11). While God sometimes challenges our assumptions about normal patterns of events (e.g., Mary's virginal conception, Lk 1:26-38), those in Scripture who encountered the Lord regularly concluded that it is more reasonable to cling to him who consistently delivers by his power and mercy (Lk 1:46-55) than to their preconceptions about the universe. All through the New Testament we find that appropriate faith is not vague belief in the divine but rather a trust in the God of Israel (Heb 11), culminating in a particular faith in Jesus Christ. This brings both great challenge and unexpected hope. This juxtaposition is exemplified by the distraught father who brings his demon-possessed boy to Jesus and cries out, "I believe; help my unbelief" (Mk 9:24//Mt 17:14-19). Jesus offers hope to those who, like this father, have not known what or whom to trust. By faith in and through Christ their horizon can be expanded and they begin to see God.

Faithful reason is chiefly a matter of relating to the triune God in humble dependence upon him. We find ourselves faith*less* when we see only pain and chaos and not the Creator and Redeemer. Yet, according to the Gos-

> We ought to seek our conviction in a higher place than human reasons, judgments, or conjectures, that is, in the secret testimony of the Spirit.
>
> John Calvin,
> *Institutes of the Christian Religion*

pels, the only way to see and understand the truth of God is by the power of his Spirit. Not only does the Spirit empower God's redemptive activities (e.g., Mary's pregnancy and Jesus' resurrection from the dead, Mt 1:18; Rom 8:11), but also it is the Spirit alone who opens the eyes and illuminates the heart to bring understanding (Eph 1:18). "When the Spirit of truth comes, he will guide you into all the truth" (Jn 16:13). What is this truth to which the Spirit testifies, whether for the apostles or Christians in general? Does the believer instantly gain mastery over all areas of knowledge? Will the Christian effortlessly solve every calculus problem? Obviously not!

Rather, the specific point of the Spirit's revelatory action is to draw people to the Father through the Son. The Spirit leads us into the truth by solidifying the memory of Jesus the Christ and drawing people to trust the crucified Lord (Jn 16:13-15; 17:17). The Spirit alone brings a person from the blinding bondage of sin to the freedom of faith and communion with God (cf. Jn 3:5-8; Rom 8:1-16). In this way, the Spirit does not work against reason, but rather the Spirit empowers us, in and through our rational faculties, to acknowledge the truth by redirecting us to the trustworthy God as he has made himself known in his Word.

We see this principle of the Spirit working with reason in the life and ministry of the apostle Paul. Playing on variations of the word *faith* (Greek: *pistis*), Paul thanks God for replacing his unbelief (*apistia*) and ignorance with "the faith (*pisteos*) and love that are in Christ Jesus" (1 Tim 1:13-15). Paul, empowered by the Spirit, was judged faithful (*piston*, 1 Tim 1:12) and able to serve as an example to those who are to believe (*pisteuein*, 1 Tim 1:16), having been entrusted (*episteuthēn*, 1 Tim 1:11) with bringing the good news to them. When proclaiming this faith before Festus, and in response to the charge that he was "out of his mind," Paul responds that he is not crazy but rather speaks with "true and rational words" (Acts 26:25). Paul's example shows us how he understood the interplay of faith and reason. Faith expands the parameters of reason without needlessly sacrificing it. As Paul says so plainly: "Why is it thought incredible by any of you that

Faithful Reason

God raises the dead?" (Acts 26:8). Given a belief in the God who creates and redeems, along with a corresponding submission to his self-revelation, Paul concludes that resurrection is a perfectly reasonable claim.

When Gregory of Nazianzus was replying to the "posers of puzzles," he employed vigorous argumentation, but always within the context of faith. He argued that faith empowers rather than confines reason:

> For when we abandon faith to take the power of reason as our shield, when we use philosophical enquiry to destroy the credibility of the Spirit, then reason gives way in the face of the vastness of the realities. Give way it must, set going, as it is, by the frail organ of human understanding. What happens then? The frailty of our reasoning looks like a frailty in our creed. Thus is it that, as Paul too judges, smartness of argument is revealed as a nullifying of the Cross. *Faith, in fact, is what gives fullness to our reasoning.*[11]

Reason we must, but always from a position of faith, rather than from an imaginary neutrality which treats faith as optional. There are no true unbelievers; we all place our trust in something. Therefore, whatever its content, our faith inescapably informs what we determine to

---

[11] Gregory Nazianzus, Oration 29.21, *On God and Christ: The Five Theological Orations and Two Letter to Cledonius,* trans. Frederick Williams and Lionel R. Wickham (Crestwood, N.Y.: St. Vladimir's Seminary Press, 2002), p. 89, emphasis added.

be reasonable. Reason is not mocked by faithful theologians; it is put to proper use as the servant of faith rather than its master.

This conclusion about the place of reason is reinforced when we consider the knowledge that is pursued in true theology. The biblical portrait of both faith and knowledge is personal and never merely propositional. When John Calvin spoke of having "knowledge of God," on the one hand he meant more than merely cognitive understanding, while on the other hand he also consistently warned about the dangers of speculation.[12] His language of "knowledge" can roughly be understood in contemporary language as "existential apprehension"—true knowledge of God necessarily affects the inner life of a person in some way.[13] Søren Kierkegaard, in his own startling fashion and through his pseudonym Johannes Climacus, states that "truth is subjectivity."[14] While some misinterpret the statement as a form of radical relativism, he is in fact reminding his readers of something Scripture affirms: one either stands in relation to "truth" or to "untruth."[15] Sin, not analytical limi-

---

[12] See, e.g., John Calvin, *Institutes of the Christian Religion*, ed. John T. McNeill, trans. Ford Lewis Battles, 2 vols., Library of Christian Classics (Philadelphia: Westminster Press, 1960), 1.5.9-10, though this theme is strongly assumed and articulated throughout the *Institutes*.

[13] See the translator's note in Calvin, *Institutes* 1.1.1 (pp. 35-36).

[14] Soren Kierkegaard (under the name Johannes Climacus), *Concluding Unscientific Postscript*, ed. Walter Lowrie, trans. David F. Swenson (Princeton: Princeton University Press, 1941), esp. pp. 169-224.

[15] For a brilliant exploration of Kierkegaard's view of truth, rea-

tations, keeps one in "untruth," and it takes the Savior and Reconciler to free one from this bondage.[16] Kierkegaard challenges us to recognize the relationship between truth and experience, between reason and emotion, between cognitive movement and existential embrace. "Christianity is concerned with how people can actualise Truth in their lives; it wants to see Truth not merely as propositions to be believed, but as something to be incorporated in the inner life, the 'subjectivity' of the individual."[17]

Faithful reason exerts itself best from within the life of worship. As Karl Barth remarked, knowing God always consists of "not mastering the object but being mastered by it."[18] God and his revelation stand over us. In the end,

---

son and faith, see C. Stephen Evans, *Passionate Reason: Making Sense of Kierkegaard's Philosophical Fragments*, The Indiana Series in the Philosophy of Religion (Bloomington: Indiana University Press, 1992).

[16] E.g., Søren Kierkegaard, *Philosophical Fragments and Johannes Climacus*, ed. Howard Vincent Hong and Edna Hatlestad Hong (Princeton: Princeton University Press, 1985), pp. 14-20, 46-48.

[17] C. Stephen Evans, *Faith Beyond Reason* (Edinburgh: Edinburgh University Press, 1998), p. 13. Cf. N. T. Wright's argument for the role of love in a properly oriented epistemology. He concludes, "All knowing is a gift from God, historical and scientific knowing no less than that of faith, hope and love; but the greatest of these is love." N. T. Wright, *Surprised by Hope: Rethinking Heaven, the Resurrection and the Mission of the Church*, 1st ed. (New York: HarperOne, 2008), p. 74. See also Cornelius Van Til, *Survey of Christian Epistemology*, vol. 2: *In Defense of Biblical Christianity* (1932; reprint, Nutley, N.J.: Presbyterian and Reformed 1969), esp. chap. 1, pp. 14-16.

[18] See Karl Barth, *Anselm, Fides Quaerens Intellectum: Anselm's Proof of the Existence of God in the Context of His Theological Scheme*, 1st Eng-

we are the ones who are under the microscope, not God. Such conclusions grow out of what we learn from Scripture. As Job discovered, standing before the Lord who posed questions of him, it is not God who must answer us:

> "Where were you when I laid the foundation of
>   the earth?
> Tell me, if you have understanding. . . .
> "Who has put wisdom in the inward parts
> or given understanding to the mind? . . .
> "Is it by your understanding that the hawk soars
> and spreads his wings toward the south?
> "Is it at your command that the eagle mounts up
> and makes his nest on high? . . .
> "Will you even put me in the wrong?
> Will you condemn me that you may be in the
>   right?" (Job 38:4, 36; 39:26-27; 40:8)

Like Job, we must recognize that our questions about God deal with matters "too wonderful" for us; we have uttered things we "did not understand" (Job 42:3). Our hope is to glimpse the glory and wonder of God, his grace and mercy, so that our lives might be bent around his reality. G. K. Chesterton memorably said, "The poet only asks to get his head into the heavens. It is the logician who seeks to get the heavens into his head. And it is his head that splits."[19]

---

lish ed., Pittsburgh Reprint Series, no. 2 (Pittsburgh: Pickwick Press, 1985), p. 55.

[19]G. K. Chesterton, *Orthodoxy* (1908; reprint, Westport, Conn.:

Theology is best understood as an art and a science—a practical science. As theologians we do not put God in his place, but we draw near to him who alone gives us our place and reveals it to us, who brings a peace that surpasses all understanding. "Faith is the resting of the heart on God," seeing him who alone is worthy of praise, prayers and hope—we trust him with our very lives.[20] Here we experience true "cognitive rest," which could be described in this context as a "godly sense of satisfaction" with what is known, even within the mysteries and questions that abide.[21] In fact, it becomes unreasonable not to exalt this eternal triune God who reveals himself as the Creator, Redeemer and Sustainer. And it becomes impossible to imagine theology that is not hungering and thirsting for communion with God.

Greenwood, 1974), p. 29.

[20]William Ames, *The Marrow of Theology*, ed. John Dykstra Eusden (Grand Rapids: Baker Books, 1997), p. 80.

[21]See John M. Frame, *The Doctrine of the Knowledge of God*, A Theology of Lordship (Phillipsburg, N.J.: Presbyterian and Reformed, 1987), pp. 152-53.

6

PRAYER AND STUDY

*Be constant as well in prayer as in reading;
now speak with God, now let God speak with you . . .*

CYPRIAN (D. 258), EPISTLE 1.15

■ ■ ■

ONE OF THE GREAT DANGERS in theology is making our faith something we discuss rather than something that moves us. We lapse into this problem when we treat God as the mere object of our study rather than as the Lord we worship. Helmut Thielicke exposed this temptation in his delightful book, *A Little Exercise for Young Theologians*. He noticed that students of theology often developed soul-starving tendencies, such as the shift from reading the Bible in the "second person" to the "third person," from seeing that it addresses them personally to treating it as an impersonal system of thought. "This transition from one to the other level of thought, from a personal relationship with God to a merely technical reference, usually is exactly synchronized with the moment that I no longer can read the word of Holy Scripture as a word to me, but only as the object of exegetical endeavors."[1] Reading Scripture merely to look for doctrinal proof texts or sermon illustrations, rather than as the blazing Word which is alive and active, kills our spirit. We should not ignore abuses of interpretation or neglect important

> True Light, assist us,
> O God the Father all powerful!
> Light of Light, assist us,
> Mystery and power of God!
> Holy Spirit assist us,
> The bond between Father and Son.
>
> Marius Victorinus
> (c. 300-370), "First Hymn"

hermeneutical principles, but at its most fundamental level, Scripture is God's voice to his people, and by his Spirit we encounter it as a living, rather than a dead, letter.

Another danger for those beginning theological studies is what Thielicke calls an "illegitimate identification with another."[2] To learn the story of Luther's personal discovery of God's radical grace is not the same thing as personally receiving that grace. Being able to speak eloquently about Søren Kierkegaard's passionate wrestling in the faith is not the same thing as embracing that faith

---

[1] Helmut Thielicke, *A Little Exercise for Young Theologians* (Grand Rapids: Eerdmans, 1962), p. 33.
[2] Ibid., p. 11.

oneself. There is a potential for confusion between factual knowledge and personal experience. If not addressed, this gap can be deadly. The popular seventeenth-century pastor Richard Baxter warned his fellow preachers that telling others to believe the gospel is not the same thing as feasting upon this reality for oneself. His warning came by way of analogy: "Many a tailor goes in rags, that maketh costly clothes for others; and many a cook scarcely licks his fingers, when he hath dressed for others the most costly dishes."[3] How sad for us to speak of God often, and yet neglect our own communion with him.

> Theological work does not merely begin with prayer and is not merely accompanied by it; in its totality it is peculiar and characteristic of theology that it can be performed only in the act of prayer.
>
> Karl Barth, *Evangelical Theology*

So how do we avoid depersonalizing our theological endeavors? How do we avoid not knowing the person we study? *There can be no substitute for prayer.* Here we speak not merely of times set apart when we fold hands and

---

[3]Cited by Paul Chang-Ha Lim, "The Reformed Pastor by Richard Baxter (1615-1691)," in *The Devoted Life: An Invitation to the Puritan Classics*, ed. Kelly M. Kapic and Randall C. Gleason (Downers Grove, Ill.: InterVarsity Press, 2004), p. 152.

bow heads, but also of a way of being. We are concerned not only to have a few minutes a day set apart for God but also to have a constant communion him (1 Thess 5:17; cf. Jn 15:1-17). Whether eating, drinking, laughing or working, all that we do is done before the face of God. This is what undergirded the Reformation slogan *coram Deo*—living before God in all areas of life. This especially applies to our theological studies. Here we are on holy ground, and thus our attitude must be an attitude of prayer. If we are to be faithful, we must always be aware of his presence.

Prayer makes faithful theology possible, but it is not a substitute for sustained theological reflection. In 1911, the famed B. B. Warfield was asked to speak on the "Religious Life of Theological Students" at Princeton Theo-

> By means of the speech of the Father in heaven his children learn to speak with him. Repeating God's own words after him, we begin to pray to him.
>
> Dietrich Bonhoeffer, *Psalms*

logical Seminary. He stated that a minister must be learned, which is why they were at seminary in the first place. If they were not educated, then they would likely become incompetent and unable to pastor with the skills demanded of those handling the Word of God. However, being well-read was not enough, since "before and above being learned, a minister must be godly."[4] What frustrated Warfield was that people pitted these two ideas against each other: *either* you were a learned minister *or* a godly minister, but you could not be both. Warfield would have none of it: "Nothing could be more fatal. . . . Recruiting officers do not dispute whether it is better for soldiers to have a right leg or a left leg: soldiers should have both legs."

Warfield adds:

> Sometimes we hear it said that ten minutes on your knees will give you a truer, deeper, more operative knowledge of God than ten hours over your books. "What!" is the appropriate response, "than ten hours over your books, on your knees?" Why should you turn from God when you turn to your books, or feel that you must turn from your books in order to turn to God? If learning and devotion are as antagonistic as that, then the intellectual life is in itself accursed, and there can be no question of a religious life for a student, even of theology.[5]

How often do we set up this false dichotomy? Theological reflection can and should be a rigorous, authentic and humble dialogue with God.

Anselm (1033-1109), the archbishop of Canterbury, ex-

---

[4]B. B. Warfield, "The Religious Life of Theological Students," in *Selected Shorter Writings of Benjamin B. Warfield*, ed. John E. Meeter, 2 vols. (Nutley, N.J.: Presbyterian and Reformed, 1970), 1:411-12. For the whole essay see 1:411-25.
[5]Ibid., 1:412.

plored questions about everything from the incarnation to potential proofs for the existence and essence of God. Modern students who read extracts from his work, however, often do not realize that he framed some of his writ-

> Be very careful, Christian friends, that no one of you be found not only not speaking with or reflecting wisdom, but even despising and opposing those who pursue the study of wisdom. The ignorant, among other problems, have this worst fault of all: they consider those who have devoted themselves to the word and teaching as vain and useless. They prefer their own ignorance (which they call spiritual "simplicity") to the study and labors of the learned.
>
> Origen of Alexandria (185-254), *Homily on Psalm 36*

ings not as logical puzzles but as extended prayers. Anselm begins his *Proslogion* by calling his readers to pray while reading, as he does while writing. His prayer gives us a model for our own studies:

> I acknowledge, O Lord, with thanksgiving, that thou hast created this thy image in me, so that, remembering thee, I may think of thee, may love thee. But this image is so effaced and worn away by my faults, it is so obscured by the smoke of my sins, that it cannot do what it was made to do, unless thou

renew and reform it. I am not trying, O Lord, to penetrate thy loftiness, for I cannot begin to match my understanding with it, but I desire in some measure to understand thy truth, which my heart believes and loves. *For I do not seek to understand in order to believe, but I believe in order to understand.* For this too I believe, that "unless I believe, I shall not understand."[6]

Anselm understood that "a theological thought can breathe only in the atmosphere of dialogue with God."[7] Our study informs our prayers, and our prayers enliven our study. We cannot choose between prayer and study; faithful theology requires prayerful study.

---

[6]Anselm, "An Address (Proslogion)," in *A Scholastic Miscellany: Anselm to Ockham*, ed. Eugene R. Fairweather (Philadelphia: Westminster Press, 1961), p. 73, emphasis added.
[7]Thielicke, *A Little Exercise for Young Theologians*, p. 34.

7

HUMILITY AND REPENTANCE

*He leads the humble in what is right,
and teaches the humble his way.*

PSALM 25:9

■ ■ ■

GOD OPPOSES THE PROUD but gives grace to the humble (Ps 138:6; Prov 3:34 [cf. the Septuagint version]; Mt 18:1-4; Jas 4:6; 1 Pet 5:5). What is it about arrogance that God so abhors, and why does he regard humility so favorably? Both of these attributes are attitudes toward God and others (Lk 18:9-14). Pride has lost sight of the gap between the holy Creator and sinful humanity, producing self-absorption and contempt for others. Humility has a vision of God's majesty, love and forgiveness in Christ, producing love for God and one's neighbors (Phil 2:1-5). How we treat others—whether living neighbors or ancient authors—reveals a great deal about how we view ourselves before God (1 Jn 3:10-17; 4:7-21).

The path of pride burdens us with defensiveness,

while the way of humility frees us to receive teaching and correction. The first path seeks self-justification, while the second pursues truth wherever it leads. We cannot engage properly in theological reflection without

> When pride comes, then comes disgrace,
> but with the humble is wisdom.
>
> Proverbs 11:2

due humility, both before God and before others. Humility recognizes one's dependence on the wisdom and insight of others.

While Augustine is commonly considered the father of Western orthodox Christianity, he never saw his own conclusions as indisputable. In response to a letter that questioned ideas from one of his books, Augustine distinguished his own thoughts from those of Scripture's binding authority. He described his theology as a work in progress, and he believed that since the goal was truthful reflection on God, he should constantly be open to revision. If he saw error in one of his conclusions, such a "mistake is *not* to be regarded with surprise or grief, but rather forgiven, and made the occasion for congratulating me, not, of course, on having erred, but on having renounced an error."[1] It is the subtlety of "self-love" that hardens us, keeping us wanting others to be wrong and

---

[1] Augustine, Letter 143.2, in *A Select Library of the Nicene and Post-Nicene Fathers of the Christian Church*, ed. Philip Schaff et al. (Peabody, Mass.: Hendrickson, 1994), 1.1:490, emphasis added.

Humility and Repentance

preventing our spiritual development. Near the end of his life Augustine put together a book titled *Retractations*, in which he looked at his own voluminous writings and revised countless claims he made earlier in his life.[2] This was a sign of strength rather than weakness in Augustine's approach. Anyone who stands at the end of his days and claims never to have changed his mind should not be

> In God you come up against something which is in every respect immeasurably superior to yourself. Unless you know God as that—and, therefore, know yourself as nothing in comparison—you do not know God at all. As long as you are proud you cannot know God. A proud man is always looking down on things and people: and, of course, as long as you are looking down, you cannot see something that is above you.
>
> C. S. Lewis, *Mere Christianity*

praised for unwillingness to compromise but rather pitied for naïve pride.

Humility reminds us that there is One far greater than us. We love and acknowledge this Lord who surpasses us in every way. Humility also bears in mind our finitude and fallenness. Our finitude constantly reminds us of our dependence on others and of the incomplete-

---

[2] Augustine, *The Retractations* (Washington, D.C.: Catholic University of America Press, 1968).

ness of our theological constructions. Theological error develops not simply out of our sin but also because there are limits to our attempts at cognitive harmony. We cannot fathom how all things work together; every time we believe our accounts are exhaustive, we inevitably discover just how much we do not know or all that we have misunderstood. No divine reality can be flatly reduced to words, concepts, images or narratives. God is never less than these, but he is more than them. The reality of God always exceeds our expressions and our understanding of them.

Despite our limits, we take our task with utmost seriousness, and we recognize that our fallen, not just finite,

> Love theology, of course: but love theology for no other reason than it is THEOLOGY—the knowledge of God—and because it is your meat and drink to know God, to know him truly, and as far as it is given to mortals, to know him whole.
>
> B. B. Warfield, "Spiritual Culture in the Theological Seminary"

nature clouds our vision. It should not be surprising, therefore, that wrestling through the teachings of the faith often changes us—our thinking and our lives—and in this way we experience the joy of repentance.

Repentance occurs not only when we recognize the

need to change our actions but also when we change our minds after discovering improper or weak thoughts regarding God. Scripture often highlights repentance in the context of dealing with idolatry; problems with obedience frequently stem from a growing divide between idolatrous ideas about God and his reality (see 1 Kings 8:48; Ezek 14:3-5; Rev 9:20-21). When the people of God found themselves clutching an idol, in whatever form, they were called to repent. They had worshiped that which was not God. For example, when King Josiah found and read the Book of the Law which had been lost, he discovered how the people of Judah had strayed from God in their thoughts and actions, and with this new knowledge came the call for repentance (2 Kings 22–23).

Revelation and repentance often come together, as God draws people to a deeper knowledge of himself. Significantly, we find that repentance is called for as people encounter the Messiah, God's revelation of himself. It is not a coincidence that John the Baptist's message of repentance is one of the few episodes included in all four Gospels (Mt 3:1-12//Mk 1:2-8//Lk 3:2-17//Jn 1:6-7). John called the people to be ready for God's kingdom and its King. Using the words of the prophet Isaiah, John proclaimed that with the coming of the Lord "all flesh shall see the salvation of God" (Lk 3:6//Is 52:10). But this was light coming in the midst of darkness, and thus required repentance. One must approach the revelation of God in humility and repentance, ready to receive what God gives rather than impose preconceived ideas. The New

Testament records many expectations held by first-century Jews that did not match the reality of the Messiah who arrived. He neither crushed Israel's political or social enemies nor restored the nation to freedom from foreign rule. The New Testament shows us that in Christ the mystery of God is made known, the hidden is revealed, and the call to a changed life grows out of an encounter with the Lord (Rom 16:25-27; Col 1:24-29; 2:2-3). Jesus conquered sin, death and hell, which were greater threats to the Jews than Rome. His victory through the cross and resurrection, rather than the sword or public policy, is an absurdity to the Greeks and a scandal to the Jews (1 Cor 1:21-25), and understanding this victory requires repentance in the form of letting God reshape our minds and hearts. The good theologian works in humility and repentance

> Almighty God, unto whom all hearts be open, all desires known, and from whom no secrets are hid: Cleanse the thoughts of our hearts by the inspiration of thy Holy Spirit, that we may perfectly love thee, and worthily magnify thy holy name, through Jesus Christ our Lord.
>
> Book of Common Prayer

because there is no other posture to take—we come as worshipers with open hearts and lifted hands. We thank God for his Son and Spirit, and we praise him that he has faithfully revealed himself to his people.

Finally, the call for humility and repentance requires the theologian to be an honest broker, about others and about self. This means we need to speak what is true, say and believe hard things and live them out amid human brokenness. Sadly, many of us think this is about telling others how they are wrong. In reality, the judgment and need for truth telling always begins not with others but with ourselves. A theologian must first be honest with self and about the realities of a fallen world; we are not faithful if we present a plastic and sanitized portrait that does not correspond to reality.

Martin Luther made a distinction between what he called a "theologian of the cross" and a "theologian of glory."[3] Luther thought that by nature we are all prone to use our theology to justify ourselves, through various "works," whatever shape they may take. His main concern with the theology of glory is self-justification based on self-deceit. Luther worried about our relentless tendency to put the best possible spin on our own motives, actions and lives, and in this way, we seek to justify ourselves before God and others. A theology of glory goes against the way of the cross. Gerhard O. Forde captures the differences:

---

[3]Note that Luther speaks not of "theology" but more personally of the "theologian." The debate between the pattern of glory or the cross is personal, about who we are, not simply what we say. See Gerhard O. Forde, *On Being a Theologian of the Cross: Reflections on Luther's Heidelberg Disputation, 1518* (Grand Rapids: Eerdmans, 1997), pp. 69-70, 81.

The hallmark of a theology of glory is that it will always consider grace as something of a supplement to whatever is left of human will and power. ... Theologians of the cross, however, operate quite differently. They operate on the assumption that there must be—to use the language of treatment for addicts—a "bottoming out" or an "intervention." That is to say, there is no cure for the addict on his own. In theological terms, we must come to confess that we are addicted to sin, addicted to self, whatever form that may take, pious or impious.[4]

Consequently, the theologian always remains a sinner and thus completely dependent on grace. Grace is not just a conclusion one arrives at, but it must be a reality woven

> It was through Pride that the devil became the devil . . .
> it is the complete anti-God state of mind.
>
> C. S. Lewis, *Mere Christianity*

into the fabric of our being. Grace is the necessary and liberating experience of the theologian living a life of humility and repentance. We cannot rightly respond to

---

[4]Forde, *On Being a Theologian of the Cross*, pp. 16-17. It should be noted that when Luther spoke of a "theology of the cross," this phrase did not exclude the value of Christ's resurrection. Luther's point was not to pit cross against resurrection; instead he aimed to highlight our ongoing need of God's radical grace over against our subtle attempts at improperly constructing views of self-improvement.

God's revelation and worship him in any other posture. Judgment, truth telling and the confession of need must always begin with the theologian. This is the path of genuine humility and repentance. This is the path of good theological study.

8

SUFFERING, JUSTICE AND KNOWING GOD

The ox knows its owner,
and the donkey its master's crib,
but Israel does not know,
my people do not understand.

ISAIAH 1:3

■ ■ ■

FAITHFUL WORSHIP must embrace not only God's highness but also his compassionate presence. It must celebrate not only God's might but also his mercy in the midst of human sin and misery. We tend to choose between the Lord's grandeur or his mercy, but we must consistently resist this choice. Simply put, a faithful theologian is someone who—like the psalmist—knows that God's glory is gracious and that his grace is glorious.

Praise the Lord!
Praise, O servants of the Lord,
Praise the name of the Lord!
Blessed be the name of the Lord

from this time forth and forevermore!
From the rising of the sun to its setting,
the name of the LORD is to be praised!
The LORD is high above the nations,
and his glory above the heavens!
Who is like the LORD our God,
who is seated on high,
who looks far down
on the heavens and the earth?
He raises the poor from the dust
and lifts the needy from the ash heap,
to make them sit with princes,
with the princes of his people.
He gives the barren woman a home,
making her the joyous mother of children.
Praise the LORD! (Ps 113)

Claus Westermann described Psalm 113 as reaching from above the impossible heights of the heavens down to a little room in a little house where a mother rejoices over her child.[1] Divine splendor and holy tenderness perfectly come together in this psalm as it calls us to praise God for his beauty, the beauty that bends from above. The main point is not God's holy exaltation or his stunning condescension considered separately, but how together they inform our praise. The psalm contradicts the common mistake of thinking that greatness and compassion-

---

[1] Claus Westermann, *The Psalms: Structure, Content and Message* (Minneapolis: Augsburg, 1980), p. 88.

ate presence are mutually exclusive. Our God shows his greatness in his compassionate presence, and thus we praise the Lord![2] This psalm anticipates what will be

> For you know the grace of our Lord Jesus Christ, that though he was rich, yet for your sake he became poor, so that you by his poverty might become rich.
>
> 2 Corinthians 8:9

most clearly manifested in the incarnation of the Son of God. Such a dynamic must inform our minds and hearts.

Since it speaks about God, faithful theology leads the theologian outward to consider God as he is revealed in his words and actions. Thus, theology must reflect God's compassion and care for us and for our neighbors. If we are to pursue theology faithfully, we must contemplate the value God places on those who are most vulnerable and in need. We must be, in a word, anthroposensitive. Knowing and loving God leads us to love those he loves and to think and write theology accordingly.

But what does it mean to know God? Biblical knowing, as we have already discussed, includes, but also goes beyond, the acquisition of information. It is emphatically and deeply relational. And, when we come to the question of knowing God, the Bible plunges us into caring for

---

[2]Thanks in particular to Justin Borger for his help on this opening paragraph.

those he cares for, and thus into living with a concrete concern for the poor, the weak and those who suffer.

The prophet Jeremiah embodies this point in a pronouncement against King Shallum, who had failed to follow the good example of his grandfather Josiah. The Lord commends King Josiah with these words: "'He defended

> For the true sufferer, the theologian of the cross has good news . . . that the Crucified has, thus, borne our very suffering, that this suffering cannot destroy God's choice about us but, rather, points to God's preference to save the weak, broken, and poor, and to resurrect the dead.
>
> Timothy J. Wengert,
> "Peace, Peace . . . Cross, Cross"

the cause of the poor and needy, and so all went well. *Is that not what it means to know me?*' declares the LORD" (Jer 22:16 NIV, emphasis added). Knowing God gives the knower a concern for the vulnerable. To know God is to love God, which results in the transference of his interests and concerns to us (1 Jn). When God's people lose this concern, God declares their theological talk and religious services empty, even offensive. This observation should sober all theologians, professional or lay: God judges our theology faithful or false by our attitudes and responses to those in need. Theology that lacks compassion and action is no theology at all.

James reminds us, "Religion that is pure and undefiled before God, the Father, is this: to visit orphans and widows in their affliction, and to keep oneself unstained

> "He defended the cause of the poor and needy, and so all went well. Is that not what it means to know me?" declares the LORD.
>
> Jeremiah 22:16 NIV

from the world" (Jas 1:27). What I always find so startling about this statement is that the text puts caring for those in need with the call to be "unstained from the world." For in truth, we in the church sometimes seek to be "unstained" by distancing ourselves from those most troubled in society, those in most need. They can become absent not only from our churches but also from our thinking, and this does affect our theology. Unlike the hypothetical orphan on a poster ("send your contribution to the following address . . ."), the real child without parents has lots of difficulties, complications and messiness. Most of the time we cannot help that child without getting ourselves messy too. Connecting ourselves to the vulnerable, the oppressed, the damaged and the suffering will connect us with their pain and trouble. Look at Jesus—he went to the prostitutes, the tax collectors, the outcasts, and it raised serious questions about his reputation. It raised questions about his theology! It should also force us to ask serious questions about his Father, whose truth and love his Son embodies. But Jesus remained unstained by taking to himself our chaos and sin.

Paradoxically, his blood cleanses us. Such a vivid image is often lost on us because we are so familiar with it—but stop and understand: we are made white as snow through the redness of his blood. This is uniquely his work, and we do not atone for others' sins. Yet we do follow the Savior, and we do follow his cross by laying down our lives for others. We are kept unstained by the world as we follow Christ, by our words and deeds, into the pain of the world. This should not simply flow out of our theology but also inform it.

Entering into the world of those who suffer inevitably brings sweat, tears, dirt and sacrifice. The paradox here is that *unless* we get involved in the messiness and brokenness of others, we risk becoming stained by the world we

> The last words that a tired, sick Luther wrote at the end of a very full and influential life were, "We are beggars—that is true." . . . To receive from God in faith is the height of human dignity.
>
> Mirsolav Volf, *Free of Charge*

seek to avoid. We respond to Jesus' call to purity not by ignoring or retreating from the sin and suffering of this world but only by confronting the sin, loving those who suffer and watching God's grace bring healing and hope amid the grief, loneliness and pain (Jn 17:15-19; 1 Cor 1:25-31; Phil 2:15). Such compassion is not just an important civic virtue; it is at the heart of our pursuit of God because it cultivates, sustains and protects us against false worship. There somehow seems to be a connection between compassion for those in need and our understanding of God's relationship to us. Active concern for the poor and needy is a core concern of our theology.

The book of Isaiah opens with words that Yahweh aims at Israel, and especially toward the religious leaders—the professional theologians of the day:

> Hear, O heavens, and give ear, O earth;
> for the Lord has spoken:
> "Children have I reared and brought up,
> but they have rebelled against me.
> The ox knows its owner,
> and the donkey its master's crib,
> but Israel does not know,
> my people do not understand." (Is 1:2-3)

What is it that God's people do not know or understand? How have they failed so seriously that God calls them "sinful," declaring that they "have forsaken the Lord" and "despised the Holy One of Israel," for they are "utterly estranged" (Is 1:4)? God cannot even tolerate their offerings, their incense, their religious assemblies and feasts. All of their acts of devotion, even with an impeccable outward appearance, have become a "burden" to him, one that he is "weary of bearing" (Is 1:13-14).

Why? Because this worship comes from a people who have divided hearts and divided minds. Although their liturgical words and temple exercises technically conform to the patterns that God had laid down, their words and actions outside the temple do not. This implies one of two life theologies: either their imagined god is lord of religion but of nothing else, or such a god does not appear to care about anything else and finds their everyday lives acceptable. Yet Yahweh tells Isaiah that such a lived theology insults and disgusts him. It renders all their religious conformity and orthodoxy offensive. They have misunderstood Yahweh by not mirroring his heart, thus turning all their actions and words into corrupted religion.

God calls on the people of Israel to repent, starting with the priests. This includes changing not just their lives but also their theology: they need to acknowledge that God is the gracious and loving Lord of all of life, not just of temple performances. And this concern is most clearly manifested by God's call to care for those most vulnerable:

> Wash yourselves; make yourselves clean;
> remove the evil of your deeds from before my eyes;
> cease to do evil,
> learn to do good;
> seek justice,
> correct oppression;
> bring justice to the fatherless,
> plead the widow's cause. (Is 1:16-17)

Listening to this, we might conclude: "Well yes, concern for the poor and justice matters, but that is something practical that comes only after we have done our theology; it is more a rational discipline, not meant to deal with such pragmatic concerns." But we cannot maintain this position because God himself will not abide such an artificial attempt to exclude ethics from the rest of theology.

Rationality and compassionate concern for others are two indispensable aspects of theology. We see this in the admonition, "Come now, let us reason together, says the Lord" (Is 1:18). How often have I heard this verse quoted for apologetic debates, urging readers and listeners to value sophisticated philosophical responses to unbelievers' concerns? It is used as a defense for the legitimacy of rigorous logical inquiry and the supremacy of Christian arguments over against the atheist. Yet God's invitation to be reasonable here does not direct us to academic argument with an atheist—it concerns a debate about whether Israel has properly ordered its *lived* theology. Isaiah is not setting out proofs for the existence of a divine Superpower. Not at all. God calls us to exercise reason that acknowledges the organic connection between our pursuit of God and our pursuit of those he loves, those who are most vulnerable. To miss this in thought and action is to miss God.

Israel claimed knowledge of God and thought they had their theology in order. They offered appropriate sacrifices according to the law, and they even fasted; yet

Suffering, Justice and Knowing God 89

their neglect of what mattered to God provoked him to reject their prayers and attempts at self-constructed humility (Is 58:3). Truly God-ward spirituality, the knowledge rightly lived, comes not simply through the repetition of religious exercises but by taking up God's concern

> He is not the high who stands over against the low,
> but is the infinite act of distance that gives high and low a place.
>
> David Bentley Hart
> *The Beauty of the Infinite*

for those who suffer. Neglect of love for our neighbor confines theology to a pursuit of personal peace, self-improvement and detached spirituality. God equates this with adultery (Is 1:21).

Good theology is public theology. God calls his people to understand and live in his extravagant love, and this inevitably includes concern for others in the public places. Just as God has set us free from the stranglehold of sin, so truly knowing God will cause us to loose the "bonds" and "straps" of the "oppressed" in order that they also may go free (Is 58:6). Spiritual bondage and physical oppression can be two sides of the same coin. Israel's theology meant that they should care for those who suffer and are disadvantaged: "share your bread with the hungry and bring the homeless poor into your house; when you see the naked, to cover him, and not to hide yourself from your own flesh" (Is 58:7). Such a response displays God's glory as compassionate, revealing him rightly to his fallen world. The majestic God is never above concern for the poor—his exaltation and condescension are bound together. As God's people pour themselves out for the hungry and afflicted they are continually guided by the Lord even as he satisfies their own desires to know and worship the true God (Is 58:9-12).

God's concern to deal with sin is inseparable from his concern for the weak, hurting and lonely. Sin, sickness and isolation are all oppressors that Christ has come to free us from. Isaiah anticipates this as a key identifying mark of the Messiah's coming (Is 61:1-3; 42:7), and this expectation is fully fulfilled in Jesus' person and work. Christ reveals that his Father has a passionate love for the poor; thus his message is distinctly good news for them (Mt 11:5; Lk 4:18-21). A major theme throughout the synoptic Gospels is the compassion of Christ, and in this way he reveals the truth of his Father to a broken world (e.g., Mt 9:36; 14:14; 15:32; 18:27; 20:34; Mk 1:41; 6:34; 8:2; 9:22; Lk 7:13; 10:33; 15:20). God exercises his lordship in a particular manner by showing special concern for the oppressed, hungry, imprisoned and physically wounded and for sojourners, widows and the fatherless. That is the character of God's reign and the cause of his praise (Ps 146). This is how we can test claims about knowing God and truth, not by a written exam but by examining one's compassion for others.

Nowhere is this point driven home more powerfully

Suffering, Justice and Knowing God

than in 1 John. The author has heard, seen and even touched God incarnate—Jesus, God with us (1 Jn 1:1-2; cf. Mt 1:23). It is Jesus whom he proclaims: through the Son we can have fellowship with the triune God (1 Jn 1:3). This is wonderful news; it is the truth John offers as the only hope for forgiveness, life and grace. Yet in his proclamation of God's mercy John also warns us that some people claim to know God, but their consistent neglect of those in need betrays an ignorant hardness toward God himself (1 Jn 3:10). Genuine concern for theological truth brings with it a concern for one's neighbor, because the true God is known by love.

> Whoever knows God listens to us; whoever is not from God does not listen to us. By this we know the Spirit of truth and the spirit of error. Beloved, let us love one another, for love is from God, and whoever loves has been born of God and knows God. Anyone who does not love does not know God, because God is love. (1 Jn 4:6-8)

Love is the hallmark of faithful worship. "We love because he first loved us. If anyone says, 'I love God,' and hates his brother, he is a liar; for he who does not love his brother whom he has seen cannot love God whom he has not seen" (1 Jn 4:19-20). For those who know God, love is the manner and context of all knowing. Speaking of God as if one were merely conveying cognitive data betrays and falsifies the speech.

God's love has a particular bent toward those most in

need: by extending ourselves toward those who are vulnerable we reflect and replicate the love that met us standing empty-handed before God. We are the poor, the wounded, the needy. When others look more poor, wounded and needy than we, we may perceive them as an inconvenience or threat. But if we neglect them in our talk about God—well, what more emphatic way is there to condemn ourselves? We are prone to lose sight of this in our theologizing, even with how much we talk about ourselves as sinners.

It would be an equal error in the opposite direction to use the importance of compassion as an excuse for reducing theological method to political posturing. Nevertheless, we are not permitted to omit this concern, lest our theology and worship become unfaithful. When we are indifferent to the oppressed we display a fundamental misunderstanding of God and what it means to know him. As theologians, therefore, we must integrate this concern into our theological reflections, allowing the call for sacrificial action to reshape our theology. A theology that contemplates Jesus will always be mindful of the depth of our own needs, and that should prompt us to "remember the poor," not as an optional extra but as a central aspect of our theological knowledge.

9

TRADITION AND COMMUNITY

To think theologically . . . one must have served a kind of apprenticeship to that long tradition—an apprenticeship that, to be sure, never wholly ends, but one that must especially occupy a good deal of one's time and energy at the beginning.

DOUGLAS JOHN HALL, "BOUND AND FREE"

■ ■ ■

THEOLOGY GROWS BEST in community. As we have already established, this should include being part of a community of faith that is actively compassionate to those in need. Such experiences shape us in untold ways. But this community orientation also means that we self-consciously seek the counsel of the saints from both the past and the present.

While the Scriptures are our only rule of faith and practice (Mt 15:3-9), God's Spirit has guided the church through the ages as it has sought to rightly understand that Word. Even conservative theologian Herman Bavinck was quick to warn against the views of some who attempted to produce a theology from the Bible alone with no guidance from the church.[1] In misguided attempts to elevate Scripture, they often mistreated God's holy Word by isolating it from the body of Christ and ignoring the insights of others. The skilled interpreter must learn crucial historical, linguistic and literary information about the diverse writings contained in Scripture and recognize that "presuppositionlessness and objectivity are impossible." In fact, "so much study and reflection on the subject is bound up with it that no person can possibly do it alone. That takes centuries."[2] This is why the Spirit guides the church as a body and not just a collection of assorted individuals. "Whoever isolates himself from the church, i.e., Christianity as a whole, from the history of dogma in its entirety, loses the truth of the Christian faith."[3] God has put us into a body, the church—for our worship is not a solo but a chorus of praise (see 1 Cor 14:26).

> Beloved, although I was very eager to write to you about our common salvation, I found it necessary to write appealing to you to contend for the faith that was once for all delivered to the saints. (Jude 3)

Let us be clear: our views of God are not shaped in a vacuum. Each of us is laden with cultural baggage that

---

[1] Herman Bavinck, *Reformed Dogmatics: Prolegomena*, ed. John Bolt, trans. John Vriend (Grand Rapids: Baker Academic, 2003), pp. 82-89.
[2] Ibid., p. 83.
[3] Ibid.

we cannot set down by ignoring. "We learn to reason as we learn, in childhood, to use words and concepts, those words and concepts that embody the way in which our society makes sense of the world. All rationality is socially and culturally embodied."[4] Part of the theologian's task is to make sure our faith does not confuse cultural contingencies with normative continuities. Geography, socioeconomics, biology, history, temperament and experience are all factors that inevitably help shape the way we think and feel.[5] For example, it has been all too common for readers of the Gospels to see Jesus as a reflection of themselves rather than understanding him within first-century Judaism. Late nineteenth-century liberal theologians saw Jesus as the great ethical teacher, while the 1960s Jesus People Movement presented him as a hippie.[6] While it may be clear from a distance that neither

---

[4]Lesslie Newbigin, *Truth and Authority in Modernity*, Christian Mission and Modern Culture (Valley Forge, Penn.: Trinity Press International, 1996), pp. 50-51. See also Peter Berger's important discussions of these ideas, especially in terms of what he calls "plausability structures," in *The Sacred Canopy: Elements of a Sociological Theory of Religion* (New York: Anchor Books, 1967); Peter L. Berger and Thomas Luckmann, *The Social Construction of Reality: A Treatise in the Sociology of Knowledge* (New York: Anchor Books, 1990).

[5]See Alister E. McGrath, *The Genesis of Doctrine: A Study in the Foundations of Doctrinal Criticism* (Oxford: Basil Blackwell, 1990), esp. pp. 152-60; Alasdair C. MacIntyre, *Whose Justice? Which Rationality?* (Notre Dame: University of Notre Dame Press, 1988).

[6]See the writings of Albrecht Ritschl for a fair representative of classical liberal theology, and although having differences with those from the Jesus People Movement, watch the film version of *Jesus Christ Superstar* (1973) to see a sampling of how Jesus was portrayed with hippie sensitivities during the late 1960s and into the early 1970s.

view is faithful to the biblical portrait of Christ, it is always difficult to see around the filters that come from one's own environment. One of the best ways to become aware of our cultural prejudices and reduce our blind spots is to spend time in the presence of the saints, especially the saints who lived in times different from our own. Effective self-criticism requires that we increase—in number and breadth—our dialogue partners to expose our preconceptions and to help us avoid pitfalls. The most important conversation partners for the theologian come from the church, both historically and locally. Let us begin with the value of engaging with tradition.

Orthodoxy should matter to all Christians. This word can be fairly rendered as right (*orthos*) praise (*doxa*). Early ecumenical creeds—those written by the universal church in the first centuries after the New Testament—were attempts to provide basic outlines of the essential

> He who marries the spirit of the age soon finds himself a widower.
>
> W. R. Inge (1860-1954)

truths of Scripture and to ensure that our praise was directed to the true God. In the view of the early church, disagreement with these fundamental (creedal) statements of the faith moved one outside the church. Christians around the world still recite the Apostles' Creed or the Nicene Creed during worship, affirming their common faith with the saints of old. The creeds remind us that God requires us to worship him in faith, which we do by receiving and acting on his self-revelation as God the Father, Son and Holy Spirit.

Since early on, however, there have been distinctions and divisions in the church, and thus there is no single universal statement that captures every aspect of the Christian faith. Differences among Christian responses to God's Word abound. How should we think about such distinctions? On the one hand, Jesus' high-priestly prayer (Jn 17:22-23) shows the importance he attributed to the unity of the church, for it reflects the unity of God. Divisions in the Bride of Christ can never be taken lightly, and unity must always be a goal of the catholic (i.e., universal) church (Eph 4:1-6). Different members of the one body of Christ (Rom 12; 1 Cor 12) will inevitably see and praise God differently. The criterion of truth amid these differences, however, requires that these various perspectives maintain faithful views of the same reality; otherwise, they are no longer Christian.

Sometimes various traditions of the orthodox Christian church (those who affirm the basic creeds) highlight different biblical truths that have been neglected or forgotten by others. For example, the Lutheran tradition will never let us forget the Pauline cry that we are "justified by faith" alone, while Anabaptists remind us to never confuse the power of the state with the power of the gospel. The Eastern Orthodox tradition teaches us to study respectfully at the feet of the early church fathers, while contemporary charismatic churches warn us against treating God's Spirit as absent from our midst. It is fair to say that each of these traditions grows out of a genuine attempt to respond faithfully to God, and thus we do well to understand them.

==Technically there is only one Christian faith with a variety of expressions (traditions):== restricting God's grace to

> Tradition means giving votes to the most obscure of all classes, our ancestors.
> It is the democracy of the dead.
>
> G. K. Chesterton,
> *Heretics/Orthodoxy*

one tradition risks pulling out the wheat with the weeds (Mt 13:24-30). But the outright opposition between some points of doctrine shows that not all traditions are equally valid. Theologians, being the limited and sinful creatures that we are, inevitably reproduce our limitations in our work. Further, every believer stands within some tradition. We often align ourselves with one group of Christians or another because they seem, however imperfectly, to be more faithful in their handling of God's Word and in their obeying of his voice in the world.

Clearly, as the author of this book, I also come from a particular theological heritage. First, I consciously identify myself within the trajectory of the universal, orthodox church, which confesses the triune God. Because I learn from the whole history of the Christian church, I view myself, to borrow a sentiment from Thomas Oden, as a *consensual theologian*—I seek to maintain an organic

> The self-giving presence of Christ in the Church is the law of theology, the reality which governs theological reason.
>
> John Webster, *Holiness*

continuity with past orthodox theologians even amid the obvious variety.[7] We agree on far more than is often appreciated. Second, I am a child of the sixteenth-century Protestant Reformation movement, which distinctly unpacked such slogans as *sola fide* ("by faith alone"), *sola gratia* ("by grace alone"), *sola Scriptura* ("Scripture alone"), *solus Christus* ("Christ alone") and *soli deo Gloria* ("glory to God alone"). Of the branches that grew in the soil of the Reformation, I locate myself particularly with the Reformed tradition, originally shaped by the likes of Ulrich Zwingli (1484-1531), Peter Martyr Vermigli (1499-1562) and the more well-known John Calvin (1509-1564). This movement, sometimes unfortunately restricted by the name Calvinism, has developed in a variety of ways and locations since that time. I am shaped by this tradition in untold ways, and I am thankful for it. But this is a living

---

[7]Thomas Oden's approach is magisterially employed in his three-volume systematic theology: *The Living God: Systematic Theology*, vol. 1; *The Word of Life*, vol. 2; *Life in the Spirit*, vol. 3 (San Francisco: HarperSanFrancisco, 1987-1992).

tradition, not a dead one. Jaroslav Pelikan helps us understand this:

> Tradition is the living faith of the dead; traditionalism is the dead faith of the living. Tradition lives in conversation with the past, while remembering where we are and when we are and that it is we who have to decide. Traditionalism supposes that nothing should ever be done for the first time, so all that is needed to solve any problem is to arrive at the supposedly unanimous testimony of this homogenized tradition.[8]

Having said that, our final authority is not a particular tradition but rather God himself—the Lord who has made himself known in holy Scripture. This means that, while we respect and listen to our ancestors, we do not accord their testimony the same weight as that of the prophets and apostles as contained in the Scriptures. As Stephen Holmes notes, "Tradition is what both links us to, and separates us from, the prophets and apostles who wrote the Scriptures."[9] If "theological dogma is always a combination of two elements: divine authority and churchly confession,"[10] then we can value tradition without elevating it to the status of sacred writings. This also reminds us that we have never completed the theological

---

[8] Jaroslav Pelikan, interview with *U.S. News & World Report*, July 26, 1989.

[9] Stephen R. Holmes, *Listening to the Past: The Place of Tradition in Theology* (Grand Rapids: Baker Books, 2002), p. 5.

[10] Bavinck, *Reformed Dogmatics: Prolegomena*, p. 31.

task, for our churchly confession is a living and dynamic response to God's Word; we must always be humble, as we said before, and revise our claims when we find we have misunderstood or misapplied biblical truth.

Just as we can gain great benefit from studying testimonies of past Christians, so we can also benefit from listening to our present communities of faith. Theologians are on dangerous ground when they try to separate theology from the life of the church—in fact, outside of fellowship with believers, one may wonder if any true dogmatics can occur.[11] John Owen put it this way:

> Living interaction with saints and believers is essential to the student [of theology]. It will sharpen, by exercise and practice, those spiritual gifts on which true gospel wisdom is founded, and that wisdom itself will be strengthened and increased by the holy practice. Such service is the essential inner nature of theology itself. It is also ordained by the gracious will and decree of our Lord Jesus Christ Himself![12]

In truth, the practice of the church shapes theology, just as theology shapes practice.[13]

---

[11] Karl Barth, *Church Dogmatics 1:1*, ed. G. W. Bromiley and T. F. Torrance, trans. G. W. Bromiley, 4 vols. (Edinburgh: T & T Clark, 1957-1969), p. 17.

[12] John Owen, *Biblical Theology, or the Nature, Origin, Development and Study of Theological Truth, in Six Books*, trans. Stephen P. Westcott (Pittsburgh: Soli Deo Gloria, 1994), p. 703.

[13] Geoffrey Wainwright, *Doxology: The Praise of God in Worship, Doc-*

An analogy of the relationship between professional theologians and those engaged in ministry may help. Ray Anderson describes a Santa Barbara fire in 1990 in which a combination of drought, wind and lots of dry brush created a disastrous inferno. More than five hundred homes were destroyed in less than two hours. Firefighters hastily arrived from all over but were sometimes forced to watch homes burn while they waited for orders from central command. The reason for their restraint was that an overall plan was needed lest the whole city burn; uncoordinated individual efforts would, in the end, bring worse disaster. Experienced firefighters followed the guidance of the command center because they trusted them, knowing that the leaders had themselves felt the flames and inhaled the smoke from fighting previous fires. But, as one firefighter noted later, if those in the command center had not been experienced firefighters, their judgment would not have been trusted. After major fires the captains always listened to those who had been on the fire lines, so that they could properly revise their theories for the next challenge. In this way, firefighting theory is fundamentally shaped and refined by those who experience the flames. Anderson summarizes, "Those who claim to be theologians . . . but do not allow their theology to be reviewed and corrected by those who experience God in burning bush and tongues of fire are like unto those who train firefighters to polish the truck but never to fight a

---

trine and Life: A Systematic Theology (New York: Oxford University Press, 1980), p. 7.

Tradition and Community

fire."[14] This is not an appeal to revise the gospel to match the whims of culture, but rather an appeal to hear the wisdom of Christian believers who daily wage the fight of faith.

In addition to bringing praise to God, the purpose of theology is to support the proclamation of the Word and the life of the church. It is a great danger to neglect the corporate gathering of God's people (Heb 10:23-25). Here we gather for baptism and the Lord's Supper, for here are God's self-identified people. Theologians with advanced academic degrees must beware of a pompousness that would dismiss their brothers and sisters in the pew. More than others, we are required to listen to, learn from and incorporate their faithful reflections into our living theology. This does not mean uncritical acceptance, but it does mean genuinely treating those who walk with God as our fellow pilgrims. These saints often see what we have missed or neglected.[15] They can instinctively detect errors missed by those sometimes isolated in their studies. Right after the apostle Paul challenges his readers to "renew their minds," he calls for sober judgment and a valuing of all believers. This means not thinking too highly of

---

[14]Ray Sherman Anderson, *Ministry on the Fireline: A Practical Theology for an Empowered Church* (Downers Grove, Ill.: InterVarsity Press, 1993), p. 17.

[15]For a wonderful model of the attitude encouraged here, see Richard J. Mouw, *Consulting the Faithful: What Christian Intellectuals Can Learn from Popular Religion* (Grand Rapids: Eerdmans, 1994); idem, *The Smell of Sawdust: What Evangelicals Can Learn from Their Fundamentalist Heritage* (Grand Rapids: Zondervan, 2000).

oneself but recognizing that there is one body with many members, and consequently it takes the whole to function properly (Rom 12:1-8; cf. Phil 2:1-5). Along similar lines, Charles Hodge encourages theologians to look to the flock of God for help discerning truth.

> Go with your new opinions to the aged children of God who have spent years in close communion with the Father of lights. Propose to them your novel doctrines, should they shock their feelings, depend upon it, they are false and dangerous. The approbation of an experienced Christian of any purely religious opinion is worth more than that of any merely learned theologian upon earth.[16]

We do ourselves and God no favors by neglecting the faithful, whether they are living or dead. Those in the pew should not lord their instincts over their pastors and theologians, but neither should such leaders neglect the wisdom in the pew.

There are limits to the proper role of tradition and practice when it comes to theological reflection. With all of the importance of tradition, it cannot stand above Scripture, nor can the experience of the church (Mt 15:1-9). We must retain Scripture's prophetic voice to speak against both tradition and experience. Contrary to classi-

---

[16]Charles Hodge, "Lecture to Theological Students," in *The Princeton Theology, 1812-1921: Scripture, Science and Theological Method from Archibald Alexander to Benjamin Breckinridge Warfield*, ed. Mark A. Noll (Grand Rapids: Baker Academic, 2001), p. 113.

cal liberal theology, George Lindbeck argues that authority resides in the church through its language and practices, which he describes as his cultural-linguistic model.[17] This model, however, weakens Scripture's ability to confront the church and the world. Kevin Vanhoozer points out that the church always partakes of "both gospel and culture," which is why church practices cannot ultimately be normative. "Neither tradition nor practice can be the supreme norm for Christian theology, because each is susceptible to error. Practices become deformed; traditions become corrupt."[18] The community of the church—past and present—always stands under the Word of God. Still, if our theology does not resonate with historical theology and within our present communities, we are standing on thin ice.

---

[17] George A. Lindbeck, *The Nature of Doctrine: Religion and Theology in a Postliberal Age*, 1st ed. (Philadelphia: Westminster Press, 1984). See also Timothy R. Phillips and Dennis L. Okholm, *The Nature of Confession: Evangelicals and Postliberals in Conversation: Essays* (Downers Grove, Ill.: InterVarsity Press, 1996).

[18] Kevin J. Vanhoozer, *The Drama of Doctrine: A Canonical-Linguistic Approach to Christian Theology* (Louisville: Westminster John Knox, 2005), p. 22.

LOVE OF SCRIPTURE

I rejoice at your word,
like one who finds great spoil.

PSALM 119:162

■ ■ ■

FROM GENESIS TO REVELATION we have a collection of ancient writings, at times delightful and at other moments perplexing, sometimes accessible and yet often strange, inviting and yet threatening, understandable and yet far beyond us. They are just words on a page, so what is it about these writings that make them so vital? Why are they so essential to a lived theology, a life lived to God? What we discover is that it is through the words of Scripture that the living God reveals himself to us. In these writings God acts upon us. By them he forms his church—corporately and individually—and shapes and sanctifies our worship.

While I will not develop a doctrine of Scripture here, it seems imperative that we close our reflections on key characteristics of faithful theology and theologians with a brief discussion about the import of Holy Writ. For our purposes, I will assume—and will not argue—that Scripture is authoritative, trustworthy and life-giving. While

> How amazing is the profundity of your words! . . . To look into that depth makes me shudder, but it is the shudder of awe, the trembling of love.
>
> Augustine, *The Confessions*

legitimate discussions and debates can be had about hermeneutics, textual criticism, and the like, these are not our concern here. However one works through those thorny issues, what I can say is that good, orthodox and worship-inducing theology must be rooted in, sustained by and continually nourished through Scripture.

Two errors regarding the use of Scripture in theology frequently tempt theologians, and the strength of the temptation depends on one's location. One of them, sometimes called biblicism, treats the Bible as a collection of verses that, like geometric axioms, can be understood apart from textual or historical contexts.[1] In this way the entirety of Scripture is treated almost as a collection of proverbs that you can pull out and plug in any-

---

[1] The Dutch theologian Jochem Douma warns about this approach, since it "is characterized by its neglect of the difference in circumstances between then (the time in which the texts being cited were written) and now." See Jochem Douma, *The Ten Commandments*, trans. Nelson D. Kloosterman (Phillipsburg, N.J.: Presbyterian & Reformed, 1996), p. 363.

where without question. This method gives little attention to the various genres, contexts and emphases found throughout the Bible. Furthermore, such Biblicism rarely treats a text in light of its place within the matrix of the organic and progressive nature of biblical revelation. Here we face the strong temptation of the traditionalist. Faithful theology cannot simply mean mindlessly parroting back the words of the Bible; we must ask questions

> What you heard from me, keep as a pattern of sound teaching, with faith and love in Christ Jesus. Guard the good deposit that was entrusted to you—guard it with the help of the Holy Spirit who lives in us.
>
> 2 Timothy 1:13-14 NIV

such as *what, why, when, how* and *to whom* as we responsibly try to make sense of the Scriptures. A respectful engagement with the divinely inspired text is needed. Here we wrestle; here we rest. In this way faithful theology is relational, recognizing that God reveals himself to us in grace but never ceases to be Lord. The faithful theologian treats the Scriptures as the yardstick of belief but never as a tool for abusive control. Subordinating our preconceived notions to the voices of the prophets and apostles, we aim to handle the Scriptures reverently and humbly, knowing that, however educated we may be, we too are children of our times and thus subject to problematic biases. Such awareness should not undermine our confidence in or dependence on Scripture, but it should motivate us to patiently seek corporate wisdom in the theological enterprise.

On the other hand, some theologians so disdain biblicism that they develop a theology that is only vaguely influenced by Scripture. They may insert an occasional biblical phrase or reference here and there, but the Bible does not serve as the beating heart of their theology. Instead, it is often apologized for or treated anthropologically, as an interesting religious text of a primitive people. Here we face the strong temptation of the progressive. Such an approach tends to manifest itself by extreme selectivity when it comes to the Bible, often openly resisting the Bible's abiding authority and legitimacy. I remember once talking to the theologian Donald Bloesch about this danger, and he gave me a good piece of advice: "When you look at a book on theology, begin with the index. See if and how they engage Scripture. If, for example, they never reference the Old Testament, then you have good reason to believe the theology they are developing is overly distant from the Scriptures and open to all kinds of problems."[2] In other words, faithful theology and worship always depend upon the Scriptures—in their entirety—as the avenue of God's voice for his people, both

---

[2]For Bloesch's thoughtful and distinctive approach to theology, see his seven-volume Christian Foundations series (Downers Grove, Ill.: InterVarsity Press, 1992-2004), esp. vol. 1: *A Theology of Word and Spirit*, and vol. 2: *Holy Scripture*.

then and now. The Bible is central because it is there that God clearly reveals himself, there that we hear the prophets and apostles testify faithfully about Jesus the Christ.

Let us conclude our discussion with three points: first, examining how God self-identifies with Scripture; second, how this ought to foster in us a love for and dependence on the Bible; and third, how the purpose of the words is to lead us to the Word.

> Sanctify them in the truth; your word is truth.
>
> John 17:17

First, *God uniquely self-identifies with holy Scripture*. When the apostle Paul proclaimed the universal realities of sin that infected not just the uncircumcised Gentiles but also the circumcised Jews, he anticipated the question: "Then what advantage has the Jew?" Paul responded without missing a beat: "Much in every way. To begin with, the Jews were entrusted with the oracles of God" (Rom 3:1-2). Israel was unique in the world, and central to their significance was their privilege to receive a record of God's words and actions. These were not viewed merely as wonderful ancient relics but as God's continued word to his people. Consequently, even if those who had received God's word were "unfaithful," that does not in any way "nullify the faithfulness of God" (Rom 3:3-4a). Put differently, the record of God's words and acts given to his people was true since it revealed the faithful Lord, even if those who received this testimony ended up hardening their hearts toward him.[3]

Through his prophets God had spoken "at many times and in many ways," and yet God has given his ultimate and climactic Word in his incarnate Son, who is the "radiance of the glory of God and the exact imprint of his nature" (Heb 1:1-3). Jesus is the incarnate Word: "In the beginning was the Word, and the Word was with God, and the Word was God. . . . And the Word became flesh and dwelt among us, and we have seen his glory, glory as of the only Son from the Father, full of grace and truth" (Jn 1:1, 14). Through the Word, God has made himself known: we respond to the Father through his Word and by his Spirit. With the ascension of the incarnate Son, we are not left without a faithful testimony to God; by the Spirit we receive the gift of the Old and New Testaments. The Old Testament anticipates the coming of the Son and Spirit; the New Testament reflects on these gifts as given.[4] In

---

[3]"The connexion between faithfulness [cf. Hebrew ʾĕmet and ʾĕmunâ] and truth [Greek alētheia] depends not on semantic considerations said to be peculiar to the Heb[rew] language, but on the fact that when God or man is said to act faithfully, often this means that his word and his deed are one. He has acted faithfully in accordance with his spoken word. Hence the believer may lean his whole weight confidently on God, and find him faithful. What is perhaps most distinctively Hebraic is the notion that even God binds himself to his word once spoken, especially in the covenant. Hence, the biblical writers speak repeatedly of the faithfulness of God, with whom word and deed are one." A. C. Thiselton, "Truth," in *New International Dictionary of New Testament Theology*, ed. Colin Brown, 4 vols. (Grand Rapids: Zondervan, 1986), 3:879 (see 3:874-902).
[4]See also B. B. Warfield, "The Biblical Doctrine of the Trinity," in

their totality the holy Scriptures dependably draw us to the triune God; here is God's chosen means of his continued self-disclosure. To know God we are called to know his Word.

In this way we recognize both the distinctions and the unbreakable links between the incarnate Word, the written Word and our reception of that Word. Thomas Oden argues that we can think of it this way: Christ is the "revealed Word," while Scripture is the "written Word." The Scriptures serve as our primary source to know the Word, with all other "sources," including tradition ("remembered word"), experience ("personally experienced word") and reason (which helps us make sense of the word) serving as secondary sources without the same authority as Scripture.[5] So what does this mean for the Christian, for the theologian? While we must always value tradition, experience and reason, we must continuously foster within ourselves a vital attentiveness to the Word of God. We should aim to be like Timothy, who from childhood was soaked in "the sacred writings, which are able to make you wise for salvation through faith in Christ Jesus" (2 Tim 3:15). This is not simply be-

---

Biblical Doctrines (New York: Oxford University Press, 1929), pp. 140-46.

[5]Thomas C. Oden, *The Living God: Systematic Theology*, 3 vols. (San Francisco: HarperSanFrancisco, 1987), 1:331. Oden goes on to navigate through some of the complex questions a simplified review like this quickly bypasses. For our purposes, the goal here is to provide a basic help regarding the multilayered discussions which surround the W/word.

Love of Scripture

cause the pages of the Bible contain important truths, but because through these truths/words the living Word meets us. Our study of the Bible is meant to build our relationship to God.

Sometimes in class I tell my students that next time they are alone reading their Bibles, they should lower their faces to just above the pages of the open book. Do they feel the warmth of God's breath, the nearness of his being? While such an exercise may sound (and be!) crazy, the point is drawn from the message given to Timothy: "All Scripture is breathed out by God" (2 Tim 3:16). When God feels distant, or when he seems unknowable, we are to turn to his Word—here he meets us, reshapes us, sustains us. Here we feel the warmth of his breath. God does indeed speak to us by his Spirit in and through this Word. We listen for God to speak to us in this Scripture by his Spirit. Yet as we handle the Scriptures on a regular basis we can forget their power. John Owen understood that the theologian must consistently remember that Scripture is a divine gift, for by it we hear God's voice and experience his presence.

> Everyone who devotes himself to the study of holy literature should keep it firmly before his mind, in all of his reading and meditation, that the all-holy God is, in a special manner, close to him as he works. Thus remembering that in His Holy Scriptures God speaks to the sinner no less directly than if He chose to employ a voice resounding from the heavens, the gospel student will be overcome with

due humility . . . and will conduct his studies with proper reverence for his Lord's power and majesty.[6]

As Christian theologians, let us encourage one another to remember that only by the Word and Spirit are the Scriptures truly living and active, so that they are always "profitable for teaching, for reproof, for correction, and for training in righteousness" (2 Tim 3:16), uniquely equipping us "for every good work" (2 Tim 3:17). As theologians, it must always be that the Scriptures, rightly handled, will be our final authority and hope. Only by the

> Scripture is God in communicative action. Therefore to encounter the words of Scripture is to encounter God in action.
>
> Timothy Ward, *Words of Life*

Scriptures can we make sure our worship and our lives are faithful rather than directed toward self-created idols.

Second, since God makes himself known through his Word, we are to cultivate a love for and dependence upon the holy texts. We find such a response exemplified throughout the Psalms. God's Word and work are tied together, demonstrating continuity from the act of creation to his sustaining of his people in the present:

---

[6]John Owen, *Biblical Theology, or the Nature, Origin, Development and Study of Theological Truth, in Six Books*, trans. Stephen P. Westcott (Pittsburgh: Soli Deo Gloria, 1994), p. 699.

Love of Scripture 115

> For the word of the LORD is upright,
> and all his work is done in faithfulness....
> By the word of the LORD the heavens were made,
> and by the breath of his mouth all their host....
> Let all the earth fear the LORD;
> let all the inhabitants of the world stand in
>   awe of him!
> For he spoke, and it came to be;
> he commanded, and it stood firm....
> The counsel of the LORD stands forever,
> the plans of his heart to all generations.
>   (Ps 33:4, 6, 8-9, 11)

God's counsel and plans are known through the received oracles of God. Since Yahweh self-identifies with his word, the psalmist praises his Word (Ps 56:4, 10). God is trusted, even amid confusion and pain, because his word can bring healing and deliverance (Ps 107:20; 130:5; 138:2). God's Word, given and cherished, was not simply meant to stimulate the memory but to enliven the heart and comfort the soul as it brought one again and again into communion with the living Word.

Psalm 119, which is the longest psalm we have, is one extended reflection on the glories of God's law as found in his Word. By storing up the Word in one's heart, God's people can be kept from sin (Ps 119:9, 11, 101). These words are to be delighted in and remembered (Ps 119:16), for they bring life (Ps 119:25, 107) and can be trusted as true (Ps 119:42, 142, 151, 160). Hope is consistently found in the Word (Ps 119:43, 49, 74, 81, 114; cf. Ps 130:5), and thus from this source comes divine strength (Ps 119:28). Against the background of Psalm 119, we can now appreciate the ideal presented in Psalm 1:

> Blessed is the man
> who walks not in the counsel of the wicked,
> nor stands in the way of sinners,
> nor sits in the seat of scoffers;
> but his delight is in the law of the Lord,
> and on his law he meditates day and night.
> He is like a tree
> planted by streams of water
> that yields its fruit in its season,
> and its leaf does not wither. (Ps 1:1-3)

The "law" of the Lord in Hebrew here is God's *tôrâ*, his teaching. God teaches us through his revealed and recorded Word. Consequently, whether we rise or lie down, are home or in a foreign land, God's Word serves as the lamp to our feet and the light for our path (Ps 119:105). Without it we remain in the dark and in desperate need. It makes perfect sense, then, how often the association with nourishment is made. "Man does not live by bread alone, but man lives by every word that comes from the mouth of the Lord" (Deut 8:3; Mt 4:4; cf. Jn 4:34). These revealed words are to be cherished, both because of their divine origin as well as because of their transformative powers. Again the psalmist:

> The law [*tôrâ*—teaching] of the Lord is perfect,
> reviving the soul;

> the testimony of the LORD is sure,
> making wise the simple;
> the precepts of the LORD are right,
> rejoicing the heart;
> the commandment of the LORD is pure,
> enlightening the eyes;
> the fear of the LORD is clean,
> enduring forever;
> the rules of the LORD are true,
> and righteous altogether.
> More to be desired are they than gold,
> even much fine gold;
> sweeter also than honey
> and drippings of the honeycomb. (Ps 19:7-10)

Only when the sacred writings are received as life-giving and life-sustaining will we be able to echo the Psalms' sentiment about God's preserved revelation.

Third, *we must never forget that the purpose of the words is to draw us to the Word and thus into the embrace of the triune God*. As people who grow to cherish and delight in the sacred writings, we must never forget their fundamental purpose: that we might know the true God and respond to him in repentance and faith, being drawn into communion with him. Strangely—but not surprisingly to any of us who end up professionally handling the Scriptures on a daily basis—there is always the temptation to make the Scriptures an end in and of themselves.

In John 5 we read of Jesus having a heated discussion with some of the Jewish leaders who were seeking to kill him because of his subversion of sabbath practices as well as because he was "making himself equal with God" (Jn 5:18). As Jesus' authority is questioned,

> Reading Scripture is like collecting pollen. Meditating on it is like making honey.
>
> Bruce Waltke

Jesus makes it clear he comes from the Father. Testimony of his unique significance, Jesus claims, not only is heard from John the Baptist, but also it has been the abiding truth witnessed throughout the Scriptures: "If you believed Moses, you would believe me; for he wrote of me" (Jn 5:46). In the midst of this heated discussion, Jesus says something that should make all of us who often handle the Bible take a deep breath: "You search the Scriptures because you think that in them you have eternal life; and it is they that bear witness about me, yet you refuse to come to me that you may have life" (Jn 5:39-40).

Jesus here reminds us that the words of Scripture are alive, not because they are intrinsically magical but because by God's Spirit they reveal the living Word and draw us to the triune God.[7] To study the words but never

---

[7]D. A. Carson writes, "Jesus insists that there is nothing intrinsically life-giving about studying the Scriptures, if one fails to discern their true content and purpose." See D. A. Carson, *The Gospel*

Love of Scripture 119

==encounter the Word is not to miss something. It is to miss everything! Studying the Bible alone, therefore, does not make one a good theologian.==

The sacred Scriptures are sacred because, by God's Spirit, these chosen means reveal God to us and draw us to himself. Here our idols are smashed and our worship

> Therefore every scribe who has been trained for the kingdom of heaven is like a master of a house, who brings out of his treasure what is new and what is old.
>
> Matthew 13:52

is directed to the Creator Lord whose beauty and love is always worthy of our praise. If the Scriptures do not take us to a fuller and richer worship of the triune God, then we have missed the purpose of the written Word. But empowered by God's Spirit and with a genuine thirst to receive his grace and know his mind, we can search the Scriptures like the Bereans, confident that here the Word is revealed once for all; here is the means by which we can know and live to God, and by this source we can test claims made about him (Acts 17:11).

Conclusion of Our Study

This book was not written from the perspective of a per-

According to John, Pillar New Testament Commentary, Accordance electronic ed. (Grand Rapids: Eerdmans, 1991), p. 263.

son who has arrived and finished the race. My prayers are weak, my pride a constant threat, my concern for the poor and those who suffer is often meager, and my struggle with faith is anything but over. I have known and continue to wrestle with suffering, doubt, weariness, hardness of heart and the constant presence of my own finitude. But I have also known joy, hope and the deepest comfort in my pilgrimage. What I describe above should be considered marks of a good theologian and theology, not because I have personally attained them but because I think they point in the right direction. I write merely as one sojourner to another.

On our journey we must not take Christian theological reflection lightly, for we are responding to and talking about the true and living God. Theological reflection is an act of worship, acted out in response to God, and thus it is, as Karl Barth memorably said, "a peculiarly beautiful science."

> Indeed, we can confidently say that it is the most beautiful of all the sciences. To find the sciences distasteful is the mark of the Philistine. It is an extreme form of Philistinism to find, or to be able to find, theology distasteful. *The theologian who has no joy in his work is not a theologian at all. Sulky faces, morose thoughts and boring ways of speaking are intolerable in this science.* May God deliver us from what the Catholic Church reckons one of the seven sins of the monk—*taedium* [weariness]—in respect of the great spiritual truths with which theology has to do. But

we must know, of course, that it is only God who can keep us from it.[8]

We enter this theological pilgrimage empowered by the Spirit of the living God and accompanied by the saints of the ages. Given our review of these issues of prolegomena (first things) I would like to conclude with a working definition of the task before us. In its most fundamental form, Christian theology is *an active response to the revelation of God in Jesus Christ, whereby the believer, in the power of the Holy Spirit, subordinate to the testimonies of the prophets and apostles as recorded in the Scriptures and in communion with the saints, wrestles with and rests in the mysteries of God, his work and his world.* This is the way of our pilgrimage. This is the path of living to God.

---

[8] Karl Barth, *Church Dogmatics* 2:1, ed. G. W. Bromiley and T. F. Torrance, trans. G. W. Bromiley, 4 vols. (Edinburgh: T & T Clark, 1957-1969), p. 656, emphasis added.

Name and Subject Index

affections, 16, 29
Alexander of Halles, 21
Ames, William, 42
Anderson, Ray, 102
Anselm of Canterbury, 19, 68, 69, 70
anthroposensitive, 47-48, 82
apistia, 58
Augustine, Saint, 21, 24, 33, 49, 53, 54, 72, 73, 104
Barth, Karl, 61, 66, 120
Bavinck, Herman, 93
Baxter, Richard, 66
Bible, 17, 56, 64, 82, 94, 107, 108, 109, 110, 113, 118, 119
biblicism, 107, 108, 109
Bloesch, Donald, 109
Calvin, John, 25, 57, 60, 99
Calvinism, 99
Charry, Ellen T., 34
Chesterton, G. K., 30, 62, 98
Christ, 24, 26, 57, 58, 76, 90, 94, 97, 99, 112
Christian, 42, 55, 57, 88, 94, 97, 98, 103, 120, 121
church, 19, 23, 43, 53, 84, 93, 94, 96, 97, 98, 100, 101, 103, 105, 106

Clouser, Roy A., 51
Cocceius, Johannes, 34, 46
Communion, 17, 20, 26, 58, 63, 66, 67, 115, 117, 121
community, 19, 48, 93, 95, 97, 99, 101, 103, 105
created, 17, 20, 22, 28, 69, 102
creating, 17, 22
creation, 17, 19, 22, 26, 27, 53, 114
Creator, 27, 57, 63, 71, 119
cross, 76, 77, 78, 83, 85
culture, 16, 18, 19, 103, 105
death, 17, 22, 23, 25, 76
divine, 16, 31, 36, 45, 46, 52, 56, 74, 81, 88, 100, 108, 113, 116
doctrine, 24, 104
fellowship, 20, 26, 46, 91, 101
Feuerbach, Ludwig, 16, 17, 19
Ford, David, 18
Forde, Gerhard O., 77
freedom, 53, 58, 76
Gilson, Etienne, 50
Gregory of Nazianzus, 33, 43, 59
Hardy, Daniel W., 18
Hart, David Bentley, 89
Helm, Paul, 32

Name and Subject Index

Hodge, Charles, 44, 45, 104
holiness, 41, 45
Holmes, Stephen, 100
Holy Spirit, 31, 43, 97, 121
humility, 46, 47, 48, 53, 71, 72, 73, 75, 76, 77, 78, 79, 89, 114
Ignatius of Antioch, 23
incarnation, 31, 69, 82
Inge, W. R., 96
James, Carolyn Custis, 17
Kierkegaard, Søren, 60, 61, 65
kingdom, 26, 75
knowledge
    archetypal, 31
    ectypal, 31
Lewis, C. S., 73, 78
Lindbeck, George, 105
Luther, Martin, 15, 41, 65, 77
New Testament, 56, 76, 96, 111
Newbigin, Lesslie, 52
Oden, Thomas, 99, 112
Old Testament, 109
Origen of Alexandria, 69
Owen, John, 35, 36, 101, 113
Packer, J. I., 23, 46
Pelikan, Jaroslav, 100

Peterson, Eugene H., 37
poor, 81-84, 86, 88-92, 120
rationality, 24, 50, 51, 88, 95
redemption, 23, 26, 27
religion, 19, 25, 44, 84, 87
resurrection, 57, 59, 76
Richard of St. Victor, 16
Simeon, Charles, 31
sin, 17, 22, 33, 43, 46, 54, 58, 74, 80, 85, 90, 110, 115
temptation, 17, 47, 64, 107, 108, 109, 117
Teresa of Avila, 24
Thielicke, Helmut, 10, 64, 65
Thomas Aquinas, 36
Vanhoozer, Kevin, 29, 45, 105
Vermigli, Peter Martyr, 99
Victorinus, 65
Volf, Mirsolav, 85
Waltke, Bruce, 118
Ward, Timothy, 114
Warfield, B. B., 67, 68, 74
Webster, John, 99
Wengert, Timothy J., 83
Westermann, Claus, 81
Wollebius, Johannes, 34
Yahweh, 16, 28, 56, 86, 87, 115
Zwingli, Ulrich, 99

Scripture Index

Genesis
12:1-4, *56*
Exodus
33–34, *35*
33:17-23, *35*

Deuteronomy
8:3, *116*
11:16, *17*
29:29, *55*
32:16-18, *18*
32:21, *18*

1 Kings
8:48, *75*
2 Kings
5, *56*
22–23, *75*

Job
32:8-9, *43*
38:4, *62*
38:36, *62*
39:26-27, *62*
40:8, *62*
42:3, *62*

Psalms
1:1-3, *116*

14:1-7, *27*
19:7-10, *117*
19:9, *27*
33–50, *53*
33:4, *115*
33:6, *115*
33:8-9, *115*
33:11, *115*
33:20-22, *28*
46:1-3, *29*
46:10-11, *29*
53:1, *27*
56:4, *115*
56:10, *115*
92:5-6, *27*
107:20, *115*
111:10, *27*
113, *81*
119:9, *115*
119:11, *115*
119:16, *115*
119:25, *115*
119:28, *116*
119:42, *115*
119:43, *115*
119:49, *115*
119:74, *115*
119:81, *115*
119:101, *115*

119:105, *116*
119:107, *115*
119:114, *115*
119:142, *115*
119:151, *115*
119:160, *115*
130:5, *115*
138:2, *115*
138:6, *71*
139:17-18, *28*
146, *90*
147:11, *28*
149:4, *28*

Proverbs
1:7, *27*
2:1-6, *27*
3:34, *71*
9:10, *27*
11:2, *72*
23:17-18, *27*

Isaiah
1:2-3, *86*
1:3, *80*
1:4, *86*
1:13-14, *87*
1:16-17, *87*
1:18, *88*

Scripture Index

1:21, *89*
7:9, *53*
42:7, *90*
52:10, *75*
58:3, *89*
58:6, *89*
58:7, *90*
58:9-12, *90*
61:1-3, *90*

Jeremiah
22:16, *83, 84*

Ezekiel
14:3-5, *75*

Matthew
1:18, *57*
1:23, *91*
3:1-12, *75*
4:4, *116*
5:8, *44*
9:36, *90*
11:5, *90*
11:27, *24, 37*
13:24-30, *98*
13:52, *119*
14:1, *90*
15:1-9, *104*
15:3-9, *93*
15:32, *90*

17:14-19, *57*
18:1-4, *71*
18:27, *90*
20:34, *90*

Mark
1:2-8, *75*
1:41, *90*
6:34, *90*
8:2, *90*
9:22, *90*
9:24, *57*

Luke
1:26-38, *56*
1:46-55, *56*
3:2-17, *75*
3:6, *75*
4:18-21, *90*
7:13, *90*
10:33, *90*
15:20, *90*
18:9-14, *71*
24:25-27, *55*

John
1:1, *111*
1:6-7, *75*
1:14, *111*
3:5-8, *58*
3:34-35, *32*

4:23, *16*
4:34, *116*
5, *117*
5:18, *118*
5:39-40, *118*
5:46, *118*
14:6, *34*
14:6-7, *36*
14:7, *24*
15:1-17, *67*
16:13, *57*
16:13-15, *58*
17:3, *24*
17:15-19, *86*
17:17, *58, 110*
17:22-23, *97*
20:31, *24*

Acts
9:2, *32*
17:11, *119*
19:19, *32*
19:23, *32*
24:14, *32*
24:22, *32*
26:8, *59*
26:25, *58*

Romans
1:18-32, *56*
3:1-2, *110*

3:3-4, *110*
8:1-16, *58*
8:11, *32, 57*
12, *97*
12:1-8, *104*
16:25-27, *76*

1 Corinthians
1:18-31, *27*
1:21-25, *76*
1:25-31, *86*
2:9-13, *43*
3:10-16, *55*
12, *97*
13:12, *35*
14:26, *94*

2 Corinthians
5:7, *32*
8:9, *82*

Galatians
5:16, *32*
5:19-21, *47*
5:22-26, *47*
5:25, *32*

Ephesians
1:18, *57*
2:20, *55*
4:1-6, *97*

5:8, *32*
5:15, *32*

Philippians
2:1-5, *71, 104*
2:15, *86*
3:3, *32*

Colossians
1:24-29, *76*
2:2-3, *76*
2:6, *32*

1 Thessalonians
5:17, *67*

1 Timothy
1:11, *58*
1:12, *58*
1:13-15, *58*
1:16, *58*

2 Timothy
1:13-14, *108*
3:15, *112*
3:16, *113, 114*
3:17, *114*

Hebrews
1:1-3, *111*

10:23-25, *103*
11, *56*

James
1:27, *84*
4:6, *71*
1 Peter
2:11, *32*
5:5, *71*

1 John
1:1-2, *91*
1:3, *91*
1:6-7, *32*
3:2, *36*
3:10, *91*
3:10-17, *71*
4:6-8, *91*
4:7-21, *71*
4:19-20, *91*
5:20, *24*

2 John
6, *32*

Jude
3, *94*

Revelation
9:20-21, *75*